| DATE | | | |
|---|---|---|---|
| | | | |
| | | | |
| | | | |
| | | | |
| | | | |
| | | | |
| | | | |
| | | | |
| | | | |
| | | | |
| | | | |
| | | | |
| | | | |

© THE BAKER & TAYLOR CO.

# Audubon's Birds of America

# Audubon's
# Birds of America

Text by George Dock, Jr.

Harry N. Abrams, Inc., Publishers, New York

Project Editor: Margaret Donovan
Editor, "Thirty Great Audubon Birds": Susan Roney Drennan
Designer: Norma Levarie

Library of Congress Cataloging in Publication Data
Audubon, John James, 1785-1851.
Audubon's Birds of America.
Consists of reproductions and a catalog of 500 engravings
from Audubon's Birds of America and G. Dock's text
from the Audubon folio.
1. Birds—Pictorial works. 2. Birds—North America.
I. Dock, George. II. Title: The birds of America.
QL674.A9      1978      598.2'97      77-18157
ISBN 0-8109-0665-1 (hc)
ISBN 0-8109-2061-1 (pb)

Library of Congress Catalogue Card Number: 77-18157

Printed and bound in Japan

# CONTENTS

Portrait (detail) of John James Audubon painted in 1848 by his sons John and Victor.
Courtesy American Museum of Natural History, New York

# AUDUBON
# AND
# "THE BIRDS OF AMERICA"

FOR HIS SUPERBLY BEAUTIFUL SERIES of 435 life-size, full-color paintings of *The Birds of America*, John James Audubon had won high praise and many honors from the foremost artistic and scientific circles of the Old World and the New, more than a decade before his death in 1851. Not until the twentieth century, however, did he finally gain universal public recognition for his art, his vision, and his contributions to knowledge. Now his name is perpetuated by hundreds of "Audubon" parks, streets, counties, and towns across America, by several species of birds, and even by a towering peak in the Rockies, as well as by the National, and scores of state and local, Audubon societies.

Why did Audubon's reputation remain so long confined to a small group of naturalists and wealthy art patrons? First of all, because fewer than two hundred sets of the costly original Havell Elephant Folio of his colored bird engravings were ever printed, followed by about two thousand sets of a later, small-sized edition.

Another factor tended to keep the artist out of the public eye. Until the end of the nineteenth century no widespread interest in birds or in nature existed in our country. The pioneers and early settlers found life too harsh and precarious for the gentle pleasures of the great outdoors. Most of them were much more deeply concerned about wresting a meager subsistence from nature than with enjoying or protecting the beauty of our wild creatures or the majesty of our woodlands, prairies, and watercourses. The teeming waterfowl, plover, robins, and other game, slaughtered by the wagon-load for the markets, were sold for pennies in every town and village.

When Audubon first came to America from France in 1803—the same year in which President Thomas Jefferson made the Louisiana Purchase from Napoleon—the population of our seventeen United States was barely six million, or about one person for every thirty people in the mid-twentieth century! Even at the time of Audubon's death, the population of the United States numbered only twenty-five million human beings.

New York City, when Audubon first arrived there, was a town of fewer than ninety thousand inhabitants. Its finest streets were veritable hog wallows, where household refuse was scavenged by wandering swine. Homes and shops were lighted by whale oil, and heated by fireplaces and stoves. Its water supply came in buckets from neighborhood wells. Its health was often menaced by epidemics. Its transportation was by carriage, horseback, or flimsy coach, usually through blinding dust or deep mud. A trip to nearby Philadelphia took two days by "fast stage." England was a good six weeks away by sea.

*1*

Hundreds of other American communities were scattered along the narrow coastal strip, pinned down east of the Appalachians, or confined close to the banks of the great rivers of the South and Middle West, and could be reached only by water or atrocious wagon roads. Peddlers, afoot or in carts, carried the few essential manufactured goods to settlers who battled the elemental hazards in more remote regions.

In contrast to the squalor and "quiet desperation" of life for the mass of men in the early nineteenth century were the immense, forbidding forests that surrounded our farms, plantations, and towns. The North American wilderness had hardly been touched during the first two hundred years of our slowly westering civilization. Ours was still largely a hostile land. Indians, endless woodlands, wide rivers, and trackless mountain ranges, great swamps and marshes blocked access to the continent beyond the Atlantic seaboard and the Gulf Coast. Our towering "jungles" and prairies amazed and enchanted foreign visitors with their beauty, but stood in sinister challenge before the settlers who fought to win the West with ax, fire, plow, and flintlock musket.

This was the America that Audubon encountered when he came here, first to manage his father's Mill Grove estate outside Philadelphia, and then to clerk in a merchant's store in Manhattan. Later, in the years when he was a trader on the Kentucky frontier, the route which Audubon often followed between Philadelphia and his backwoods store and gristmill took him through the wooded Alleghenies by horseback and pack train to Pittsburgh and then by raft or riverboat down the Ohio to Louisville and Henderson. His eastern point of embarkation was an obscure riverside village which gained world fame only in our day. This was Shippingport, now the site of America's first large commercial plant for generating electricity by atomic power. Thus, a bare century-and-a-half spans the distance from the glory of our primeval forests to the miracle that has harnessed the energy of the sun.

Greater still is the change that has come about among the wild creatures that once occupied our land. During Audubon's lifetime, billions of passenger pigeons continued to darken the sky in their wanderings over much of North America. Tens of millions of buffalo blanketed the western plains. Audubon was among the first to warn his countrymen against the desolation that would surely follow their reckless elimination of forest and grass, bird and beast in the swift invasion of a continent.

The destruction not only kept on, but rapidly accelerated as our population tripled in the latter half of the nineteenth century, and farms and cities replaced the wilderness. Today, only a few thousand buffalo survive on isolated reservations. The passenger pigeon, heath hen, and Carolina parakeet, once so abundant, are gone forever. So are the great auks of the North Atlantic, and the wintering Labrador ducks on our eastern seaboard. Many of our other birds and other animals, common over vast regions in Audubon's day, are now doomed to extinction or are so reduced in numbers or territory that few people ever see them outside of zoos, museums, and pictures in books.

Since the beginning of the twentieth century, a steadily growing number of people have turned nostalgically to our fast-disappearing wild places and their creatures. As Audubon had immortalized them long before, with his magic brush, observant eye, and dramatic pen, the people turned to his pictures in order to find them again.

The surge of public interest in Audubon since 1900 has been spurred, of course, by other rowels than the galloping threat to our wilderness. Among these were the organization of the various Audubon societies, begun in 1886, and inspired later by the clarion calls by which President Theodore Roosevelt aroused America to the urgency of conservation and wildlife protection, and the rising tide of popular interest in amateur nature study.

Beyond these factors, and perhaps as important as any of them, was the amazing progress of the graphic arts in recent decades, which made possible for the first time the reproduction of Audubon's *Birds of America* with magnificent fidelity in books and prints, priced within the means of most people.

The same advances in printing that made Audubon's work available to the general public created a spate of well-illustrated, inexpensive bird guides, which have expanded popular interest in bird identification and in American ornithology.

No notable bird painters had appeared in America before Audubon's day, with the exception of Mark Catesby, before the American Revolution, and Alexander Wilson, who died in 1813. Nearly fifty years were to pass after Audubon's death in 1851 before another nature artist successfully emulated him. This genius was Louis Agassiz Fuertes (1874–1927), whose paintings illustrate many of the finest ornithological works of our own generation. Fuertes' death in a motor accident cut short a career that might have made him by far the greatest of Audubon's followers. To this day, however, no naturalist is more frequently quoted, even in contemporary bird books, than Audubon in his written observations of nearly five hundred species.

No other artist ever created so great a treasure of the vanishing pageantry of our wildlife as his *Birds of America*. These paintings include most of the birds that remain with us, and all of those that have become extinct since colonial times. No man has given us so comprehensive a series of life histories of those birds as Audubon in his three-thousand-page *Ornithological Biography*. Few travelers of his time have left to later generations more vivid chronicles of frontier life than the exciting "Episodes" which intersperse the pages of that *Biography*, and the two thick volumes of letters and journals which Audubon wrote in the course of his expeditions after 1825. His paintings of the *Viviparous Quadrupeds of North America*, undertaken late in his life, with the assistance of his two sons, would entitle him to important rank as a nature artist. He also added more than forty new species to the known list of American birds.

Audubon invented an ingenious method to give dynamic life and accuracy to his paintings. He seldom worked from memory or from mounted specimens, and practically never from captive living birds. His procedure was to wire a freshly collected bird into a characteristic, lifelike position, just as he had watched its species in the wilds—singing, courting, feeding, defending its nest, in flight, or at rest or play. The wired bird was then posed against a sheet of paper marked into gridiron squares, like those on his drawing paper.

"My plan," he once wrote, "was to form sketches in my mind's eye, each representing each family in their most constant and natural associations, and to complete those family pictures as chance might bring perfect specimens." The resulting paintings astonished the artistic and scientific world by their faithfulness to living birds.

Reptiles, mammals, and insects also enliven Audubon's pages. Whip-poor-wills chase moths and a caterpillar. A barred owl alights silently beside a doomed squirrel. A whooping crane seizes a baby alligator. In most of his groupings, Audubon pictured the many facets of nature as he saw it—ptarmigan among their native Labrador tea plants, goldfinches on pink thistles, cardinals on wild almonds, and Carolina parakeets on cockleburs.

"The woods I trod," Audubon once said, "contained not only birds of richest feathering, but each tree, each shrub, each flower attracted equally my curiosity and attention." His paintings,

Audubon drew this spirited sketch of a loon in the
margin of his journal for November 1820

indeed, are as notable for the beauty and accuracy of the floral settings as for the birds. Meadowlarks crouch beneath the golden blossoms of a false foxglove. Tiny kinglets flaunt their fiery crests in a laurel. Gnomelike screech owls preen themselves on pine boughs. Pileated woodpeckers wrangle among wild-grape leaves on a dead stump. A tulip tree shelters an oriole family in its branches.

The smaller birds are sometimes completely overshadowed by the vivid colors of the flowers, like the flycatcher in Audubon's magnolia, or the swamp sparrow hiding near the blossom of a May apple, but usually there is a nice balance between subject and background—brilliant warblers in flaming azalea, bluebirds on mullein tips, hummingbirds in a scarlet trumpet creeper. Some of the backgrounds, indeed, are of historic interest. For example, the setting of the Bachman's warbler is the foliage of the famous "lost tree of Bartram," on the Altamaha River. Audubon's birds are a delight to the botanist. More than two hundred different plants are shown in *The Birds of America*.

Throughout his life, Audubon spent every possible hour observing the outdoor world. Even when prostrated by seasickness on his voyage from New Orleans to Liverpool in 1826, he still could take delight in the sight of dolphins "burnished gold by day, bright meteors at night" around the ship, and the falcon hurtling into the rigging to catch a wind-lost bobolink that came to rest there, far at sea.

It was Audubon's droll custom to relate the diverse personalities he met, and the emotions he experienced, to his observations of nature. Thus, he watched a plump servant girl "tripping as briskly as a plover" down a street in an English town. In suspense that lasted for weeks, he awaited the verdict of French officials on their purchase of a set of his prints, feeling "like a blue heron on the edge of a lake, the bottom of which the bird cannot find, nor even know whether it may turn out to be good fishing." "A full-grown man"—a lackey in red and black—recalled the scarlet tanagers of America. The Earl of Kinnoul he described as "a small man, with a face like the caricature of an owl." A famous English judge wore a wig that, in Audubon's words, "might make a fine bed for an

Osage Indian during an entire cold winter on the Arkansas River." A French girl in frills "soared aloft like a frigate pelican over the seas," to clamber to her seat on top of the London-Dover coach. From a dinner in one of the colleges at Cambridge, the *Journal* tells us, the students gradually drifted away "in parcels, as vultures leave a carcass."

Invited to a London home for a Saturday evening, Audubon absent-mindedly arrived on Friday, and "felt as much ashamed of myself as a fox who has left his tail in a trap." Eager to enjoy the sunrise view of Newcastle-on-Tyne from Isbet Hill, Audubon leaped from his bed before dawn "like a hare from plowed ground at the sight of a greyhound."

"That the Creator should command millions of diminutive creatures to cross immense spaces of country more congenial to them than this, in order to people this desolate land, and enliven it by the songs of the feathered musicians for two months at most, and by the same command induce them to abandon it almost as suddenly, is as wonderful as it is beautiful."

Audubon thus penned his thoughts on bird migration in his *Journal* one day in 1833 as the fog of Labrador lifted around his little ship to reveal clouds of birds swarming over the sea and the barren hills. He was far from the first, or the last, to find beauty and mystery in such a sight. From the quail of the Israelites in the wilds of Sinai thirty-five hundred years ago, down to the modern tragedies of migrating birds crashing against a city skyscraper in the night, men have recorded amazement at the great seasonal drama of migration. Bird migration, incidentally, was among the worst obstacles Audubon faced in his work, because he was forced to consider the widely differing travel schedules of all his models. His expeditions in search of specimens had to be precisely timed to catch the migratory birds in their brief seasonal sojourns in areas from Key West to Canada.

Many of those creatures move swiftly, and remain only a few days or weeks each year in any of the regions that Audubon could reach. Of the hundreds of species he painted, the great majority are migratory, their winter and summer haunts separated by many dangerous air miles.

In Labrador in summer he found the Arctic tern, whose yearly travels reach almost from pole to pole. Nesting up to the northern limits of Canada, these black-capped voyagers move south in September, then cross the Atlantic to France, to skirt the western shores of Spain and Africa, and winter over lonely far-southern seas—eleven thousand miles from their homes.

The smallest of all Audubon's subjects, the ruby-throated hummingbird, is a hemispheric traveler of amazing competence. Raising their broods as far north as southern Canada, these tiny jeweled thunderjets travel over a thousand miles in September, to winter from Mexico into South America. Some of them may even make the 500-mile nonstop flight across the Gulf of Mexico.

Even more remarkable are the migratory customs of some of Audubon's other birds. In the autumn the eastern golden plover leaves the Canadian Barren Grounds to fly hundreds of miles southeastward to the Maritime Provinces. From Nova Scotia they make a prodigious flight of twenty-four hundred miles or more over the open ocean to South America. They may well have been the "land birds" sighted far at sea by Columbus, which helped him to persuade his mutinous crews to sail on. The birds led him to shift his course southwestward to follow them, and thus to discover the West Indies but to miss Florida.

The gray-cheeked thrush spends our winter in Peru, Colombia, and Venezuela, and seldom arrives even in our Gulf states before late April. A short month later, however, it begins its family activities in Alaska and eastern Siberia, after a four-thousand-mile transcontinental mission and a final spurt of 130 miles a day for several days.

From boyhood, art and nature were Audubon's compelling interests. Observing on one occasion clouds of chimney swifts pouring noisily into and out of a hole near the top of a huge sycamore, the youthful Audubon chopped a doorway into the base of the tree. Entering it with a lantern at night, he first carefully counted the number of drowsing swifts that clung to a square foot of inner wood, and then measured the whole area of the hollow trunk, to report that at least three thousand birds spent the night in that refuge.

The mysteries in the life of John James Audubon have caused debate and invited exploration for more than a century. Even in his own lifetime his birth was a matter of speculation in the colorful legend that he might be the lost Dauphin of France—son of the guillotined Louis XVI and Marie Antoinette—and that he had been spirited to the New World for safety. That fantastic myth was not finally demolished until a few years ago.

From his infancy in France, Audubon showed extraordinary interest in drawing and in natural history, which he combined by sketching birds on his father's estate. From the age of fourteen until the end of his active life he was a serious collector and painter of birds and other animals. The great enigma of Audubon is not his ancestry, but the aimless, futile, and meandering course of his career well into his middle age. He had been encouraged by his parents in his pursuit of art and nature. He was trained in painting by one of the foremost French artists. Yet from 1803, when he reached America, until 1819, he forced himself to follow commercial paths for a living, rather than art—sixteen lost years of frequent failure in one misguided venture after another.

What delayed fuse of pride, despair, or genius finally drove Audubon to grasp and then to carry out his mission of painting *The Birds of America*? Once he recognized his goal his work went ahead at great speed considering the immensity of the task and the obstacles at every step.

Audubon's father, Jean Audubon, and his paternal grandfather, Pierre, had been French seafaring men in the heroic tradition of the Breton fishermen, who were sailing small boats on voyages far out over the Atlantic centuries before Columbus found the New World. Their lives were spent mainly on the decks of vessels they commanded on fishing and trading expeditions, or in combat against the enemies of France, against the pirates who haunted the old sea lanes, and in the great storms that sweep the northern oceans.

To these sturdy, courageous men, John James Audubon owed the iron constitution and the valor that were to carry him through a long career of hardship and danger. From them he may well have inherited his taste for travel and adventure as well as his alert eye for the dramatic side of life.

Pierre Audubon came from the village of Les Sables d'Olonne, on the coastal marshes of the old province of Poitou, about fifty miles south of Nantes. Owner of a vessel at an early age, he made many Atlantic crossings and coastwise trips during the first half of the eighteenth century.

In 1757, he attempted to deliver a cargo of war material for the defense of Cape Breton Island against the British. His ship was forced to surrender after a battle in which his son, Jean, then a cabin boy of fourteen, was wounded. The lad was captured, and spent five years in prison in England.

Upon his release at nineteen, Jean Audubon returned to the sea and made four fishing voyages to Newfoundland before 1768. Two years later, he entered the French merchant marine. By the time he was twenty-one he commanded a vessel, and at twenty-five he owned a fleet engaged in the French West Indies trade. After 1775 he faced the dual risks of capture by British warships fighting the American colonists and their allies or by corsairs prowling the trade routes to the West Indies.

In 1779, he was forced to give up his vessel in combat with four British ships. Once more a prisoner, he was held for a year in New York City, but was set free in time to command a French corvette under Admiral De Grasse at the siege of Yorktown, which ended with Cornwallis' surrender in 1781.

John James Audubon was born in 1785 in San Domingo, now a part of western Haiti, where his father owned a plantation. He was barely four years old when Hispaniola was overwhelmed by bloody uprisings in which over half a million African slaves slaughtered or expelled their thirty-five thousand European owners. Audubon's father escaped with his infant son and daughter, and fled to their ancestral home near Nantes, on the lower Loire.

During the younger Audubon's childhood, Nantes was a battleground between the Royalists and their sympathizers and the ultra-Terrorists under the brutal Carrier. In 1794 alone, more than nine thousand people were butchered in the little city, while countless others were drowned by the revolutionists, or died of pestilence. Such was the background that from early childhood wove the red thread of courage into Audubon's character. He was only ten years old when the Napoleonic era began. The nation was in turmoil, its school system in chaos, but the boy vastly preferred the outdoors to a classroom, and his indulgent stepmother encouraged his truant rambles in the Vendée countryside. Small wonder that, years later, he remarked that the only school he ever attended was "that of Adversity, where my tuition had been prolonged and elaborate."

"Revolutions," Audubon's father once said to him, "too often take place in the lives of individuals. They are apt to lose in one day the fortune they possessed. But talents and knowledge, added to sound mental training and assisted by honest industry, can never fail us or be taken from one who is the owner of those valuable resources."

Sentimental legend holds that Audubon was the "genius, self-nursed, self-ripened, and self-tutored among the inexhaustible treasures of the forest" that a Scottish admirer once called him. There is some basis for the myth, but his father saw to it that he was given early grounding in mathematics, geography, fencing, and music. His instruction in art was brief, and in biology, informal. In Nantes the lad spent much of his time wandering in the fields and forests with Dr. Charles D'Orbigny, who was not only the Audubons' family physician, but one of the leading French naturalists of his time. With D'Orbigny, Audubon learned about the birds, leaves, and flowers, and began to collect and paint them. No one left a deeper impression upon Audubon's later life than Dr. D'Orbigny, two of whose sons became distinguished scientists. The eldest, Alcide, was an early authority on the animal life of South America and the greatest French paleontologist of the nineteenth century.

Audubon's art instruction, though limited in time, was given him by one of the foremost painters and most dynamic teachers in the history of art—Jacques Louis David. As preparation for the difficult work that Audubon was destined to undertake, those few months in Paris with David counted for more than many years of guidance under a less exacting master.

David's stature both as artist and diplomat is suggested by the fact that he served as court painter both to Louis XVI and to Napoleon. He was not only the teacher of such future immortals of the Louvre as Ingres, Girodet, and "Gérard, painter of kings, king of painters," but also the craftsman whose brush executed such masterpieces as *Socrates Drinking the Hemlock, Mme. Récamier, The Oath of the Tennis Court, Napoleon Crowning the Empress Josephine,* and other paintings and sketches which hang today in the world's leading art museums and private collections. Delacroix named David "the father of the whole modern French School" of his own period.

Any artist accepted as a pupil at David's studio was relentlessly drilled in draftsmanship—the pencil before the palette, the line before the brush. Accurate, dramatic—even heroic—rendering of the subject in form, depth, and detail was the essence of his style. That principle was to prove as useful to Audubon in delineating every feather of a bird, and in displaying the bird in spectacular activity, as it was to David in giving dramatic realism to his scenes of ancient Greece and Revolutionary France. As Ingres said, "*Drawing* is the first of virtues in a painter—it is the foundation—it is everything."

One of our leading American bird artists, Roger Tory Peterson—painter, scientist, photographer and author—has paid this tribute to Audubon's unique place: "Audubon had one great advantage over most of the other early bird painters—the benefit of artistic training. When in Paris, he studied under the greatest French master of the day, David. In that fortunate circumstance probably lies the background of his power. Artists universally recognize in Audubon a genius that has not dimmed with time. . . . One of the things that sets Audubon apart is his success in *dramatizing* birds."

In a more technical sense, too, David gave Audubon two useful secrets that he might never have come upon by his own unguided experiments. One of these was to mark off the drawing paper in ruled squares, to simplify the sketching of outline in true proportion. The other device was David's use of the flexible manikin, the forerunner of Audubon's own invention of wiring his dead birds in natural, lifelike positions.

A far more subtle impact of David upon the future "American Woodsman" may have come from the master himself and from Audubon's fellow students in the crucible of those post-Revolutionary times in France. It was their "pride and boast to be the instruments of Destiny" in their dedication to the twin deities of Art and Truth.

Audubon's high stature as an artist, as contrasted with his reputation simply as an early naturalist, was expressed by several of his own artist contemporaries—by Cuvier, Sir Thomas Lawrence, and Gérard in the Old World; and by Vanderlyn, Titian Peale and Rembrandt Peale, and Thomas Sully in the New.

Full recognition of Audubon's position in the world of art, however, awaited the twentieth century, and Fuertes' precise, authoritative summary: "What a monumental thing—to stem the tide of adversity—to negotiate the great *Folio* reproduction—to perpetuate the evanescent beauty of bird or flower. The overpowering virility of Audubon is shown in the instantaneous attitudes and dashing motion of his subjects." As Sacheverell Sitwell asserted in *Fine Bird Books–1700-1900*, "Audubon is the greatest of bird painters. He described things that human eyes will never see again."

In 1803, when Audubon was eighteen, he was saved from being drafted into Bonaparte's forces when Jean Audubon sent him to manage his Mill Grove estate near Valley Forge, Pennsylvania. En route, young Audubon was struck down by a high fever; he was nursed back to health by a Quaker family in New Jersey. When he finally reached Mill Grove, he quickly entered into the agreeable social life, the hunting and fishing expeditions and other diversions of the American, English, and German property owners who lived nearby.

One of his Pennsylvania neighbors wrote of him, "Today I saw the swiftest skater I ever beheld. Backward and forward he went like the wind, even leaping over air holes fifteen or more feet across. A handsomer man I never saw. His eyes alone command attention. His name, Audubon, is strange to me." One winter afternoon, he joined some of his neighbors on a duck shooting and

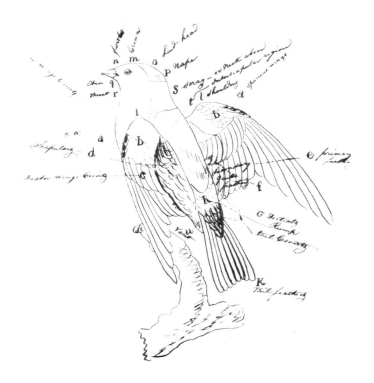

This detailed drawing from Audubon's journal for 1820–21 reveals his painstaking study of bird anatomy

skating party up the Perkiomen, near Mill Grove. Returning at racing speed at dusk, Audubon was in the lead, traveling too fast to avoid a stretch of open water in midstream. Carried along beneath the ice, he nearly drowned, but fate brought him to the surface at another air hole, from which he crawled to safety.

Even during his first months in America, he began to study, collect, and paint the wild birds and other creatures of his newly adopted country. At that time he made one of the classic, early, successful bird-banding experiments, to prove the homing instinct of birds returning in the spring from warm lands. In 1804, he developed a technique for "tagging" birds by fastening rings of fine silver wire around the legs of nestling flycatchers; some of these banded birds returned the following spring from their southern winter range.

Mill Grove was not without its romantic side. Young Audubon soon fell in love with Lucy Bakewell, daughter of a nearby English plantation owner. In 1805, at the age of twenty, seeking his father's assent to the match, Audubon returned to France for a year.

In 1806 Audubon came back, not to Mill Grove, but to New York, to work as a clerk in a Manhattan commission firm. There he met Dr. Samuel L. Mitchell, a leading physician, United States senator, and collector of birds and other animals. Audubon's mastery of taxidermy, so vital to his later work, was learned by preparing skins and mounted specimens for Dr. Mitchell, whose influence and encouragement proved useful to the artist in many other ways in later years.

In April 1806, on his way back from France, danger struck close to Audubon when his ship was attacked and boarded by the notorious British privateer "Rattlesnake." Several sailors were removed and most of the ship's provisions. A few days afterward, the vessel ran into a full gale, and was stranded in Long Island Sound.

In 1807, Audubon, with Rozier, a French associate, embarked on a trading enterprise in Henderson, on the Kentucky frontier. Audubon went back the next year to Mill Grove, to marry Miss Bakewell and take her to the wilds of Kentucky. During the journey she escaped serious injury when their coach overturned in the Pennsylvania mountains, and they drifted down the Ohio River from Pittsburgh on one of the crude flatboats of that era.

A prophetic incident occurred in Audubon's life in 1810, when a Scottish weaver, emigrant, poet, teacher, follower of Robert Burns, artist and naturalist, appeared at Henderson seeking subscriptions to his unfinished series of illustrated books on American birds. This brave, versatile man was Alexander Wilson, one of the foremost early ornithologists in the United States.

He displayed his drawings to Audubon who, in turn, showed Wilson some of his own bird pictures, and took him on a few collecting trips in the nearby wilderness. For the first time, the young Frenchman realized that there was a market for such paintings as he enjoyed creating. Yet it was ten long years after Wilson's trip to Henderson before Audubon began to follow in his footsteps as a professional bird painter—and twenty-eight hard years before his own *Birds of America* was completed.

One of Audubon's narrowest escapes from death is said to have occurred at this time. He was traveling on foot from the distant Mississippi to Henderson, enjoying the beauty of the flowers and the gambols of fawns until night came on. Seeing a light, he reached a cabin where a hideous crone allowed him to remain with a wounded Indian as a fellow guest. Their hostess showed interest in his watch and gold chain while the Indian silently warned him that he was in danger. Hardly had Audubon retired to a pile of bearskins before the woman's two sons arrived dragging a buck they had just killed. While the three squatters whispered about Audubon's watch, the woman honed a long carving knife to a sharp edge. She quietly came toward Audubon's bed while her sons talked with the Indian. At this critical instant, two other travelers arrived at the cabin, well armed. They quickly assessed the situation, and helped Audubon and the Indian to bind the criminal trio, and prepare them for "frontier justice."

The series of great Kentucky earthquakes of 1811–1812 convulsed large areas, and one of them found Audubon crossing the Barrens alone on horseback. His mount "fell a-groaning piteously, hung his head, spread out his four legs as if to save himself from falling, and stood stock still." The trees were uprooted, the earth rose and fell like the waters of a lake. Audubon expected the ground to open up and engulf him and his surroundings into the abyss. The tremors ended, however, and the horse recovered his footing and galloped along the trail, unafraid.

On one of his trips to Philadelphia for new stock for his backwoods store, Audubon was making the return ride on his mustang, Barro, when he was overtaken along the Juniata by another traveler on an equally superb horse. The stranger was Vincent Nolte, a Hollander, then building his fortune as a New Orleans importer. Their chance meeting was to bear very important fruits for Audubon fourteen years later, when the most powerful lever in bringing himself and his paintings to the attention of British scientists and men of means was the letter of introduction which Nolte wrote to the Rathbones of Liverpool, one of the most influential families in the north of England.

From other such horseback encounters came many another of Audubon's warmest friendships, and some of his most tragic experiences as well. Among the latter was his business clash at Henderson with an older brother of the English poet, John Keats. George Keats lived for a time in the Audubon home, and bought a river boat and a cargo of merchandise from the artist. The vessel soon sank, leaving Keats penniless. He wrote to his poet-brother for help, which eventually came, enclosed in a letter in which the author of *Endymion* displayed considerable talent for vitriolic prose, with Audubon as its target.

Finally, in 1819, after years of struggle as a tradesman, Audubon himself went bankrupt in Henderson. During the final crises of his business afflictions, legal difficulties also arose between Audubon and one Samuel Adams Bowen, over possession of a small steamboat that had been built by an engineer at the Audubon gristmill. Bowen not only swore that he would kill Audubon, but even attacked him with a club when Audubon had a crippled right arm. Wielding a knife with his left hand, he stabbed Bowen, and was called in for trial. Fortunately, Judge Broadnax grasped the situation, for he left his bench and came to the prisoner's dock to say, "Mr. Audubon, you have committed a serious offense, an exceedingly serious offense, sir—by failing to kill the rascal."

During the War of 1812, Audubon was a Kentucky backwoods storekeeper, more active with his fowling piece in the nearby woods than with his ledgers and inventories. The depression of 1819 drove him into jail for debt, but it also forced him to great achievement. For at last, he abandoned business, at which he had been a chronic failure, and began his immense task of painting. He actually reached fame and fortune by that solitary path in the midst of the panic of 1837, which ruined millions of his fellow Americans in the wreckage of a vast currency inflation and the collapse of a land boom.

Audubon's great work probably would never have even been launched on its way had it not been for the inspiration given him by his wife, Lucy. Without her, he might well have been content to remain the inept, indolent businessman, the carefree bird watcher, the tireless hunter that had brought him ridicule and bankruptcy at the age of thirty-four.

Only seven years later, thanks mainly to her, he had suddenly become the "American genius," hailed by art critics in Britain and on the Continent as the foremost nature painter of his time. As Mozart remarked, under quite different circumstances, Audubon might have told his wife, "If, some day, people may say that *I* had genius, *you* will know why!" Through Lucy's support, devotion, and financial help, he became an immortal.

In 1819, Audubon was bankrupt, imprisoned for debt, stripped of everything but his clothes and a gun, while his wife and children were dependent upon the kindness of neighbors. Released from jail, Audubon fell back, as a last resort, upon the art he had learned from David in a Paris studio seventeen years earlier, but had nearly forgotten—the ability to draw accurately from life. In his own story of his career, he relates the sequel: "To be a good draughtsman in those days was to me a blessing...I at once undertook to take portraits of the human 'head divine' in black chalk and, thanks to my master, David, succeeded admirably. I commenced at exceedingly low prices, but raised them as I became better known in this capacity."

Audubon's fortunes turned upward from that moment. He was soon able to give more and more of his time to his "soul-engrossing passion" of painting the wild birds of his adopted land. In barely six years after his escape from poverty, disgrace, and despair, he had filled his portfolio with more than two hundred paintings of birds. After his term in the debtor's prison, Audubon's first post was that of a poorly paid taxidermist in a Cincinnati museum. Then he began to draw portraits of local citizens, and decorate the "parlors" of Ohio river craft, and teach art in a school for young ladies.

All these ventures produced so little money that Audubon opened an art academy of his own. This did not prosper either, but it brought him as a pupil a youth of thirteen, Joseph R. Mason, whose skill in painting flowers and plants was to make him a valuable collaborator in supplying the floral backgrounds of *The Birds of America*.

Audubon and young Mason went down the Mississippi to Natchez and New Orleans, where they worked through the winter, painting many new birds, and eking out a bread-and-cheese subsistence from portrait assignments. In this project, Audubon found welcome help among several new friends in the local art colony, and especially from the celebrated portraitist, John Vanderlyn, himself a former pupil of David. Vanderlyn's painting of Andrew Jackson for the New York City Hall was completed, in fact, with Audubon posing in Old Hickory's uniform and boots, after the General had tired of standing before the easel.

Audubon now began to get good fees for his portraits—not always in cash. One of his subjects, he related, was a beautiful widow, Mme. André, who told him to buy at her expense the finest gun he could find in New Orleans. At the lady's order, the $125 percussion-cap fowling piece was engraved with the words, "Refuse not this gift from a grateful friend." He referred to this weapon as his "souvenir gun," to distinguish it from his earlier flintlock, "Tear Jacket." To a man whose living depended on shooting thousands of birds of hundreds of species, a good gun, like a faithful dog, was a cherished friend and deserved a name.

Embarked at last on the great creative phase of his career, Audubon and his wife found employment as teachers, dividing a curriculum of French, drawing, fencing, dancing, music, and the three R's for the children of a few wealthy planters in northern Louisiana. Four of the artist's most productive years were spent thus in the bayou and hill country of West Feliciana Parish. There, he painted more than a hundred of the 435 pictures later published in *The Birds of America*.

On one of his Louisiana collecting trips, Audubon was returning to his camp with a pack filled with dead birds, his heavy gun, and other equipment when he was stopped by an invisible stranger, who cried "Stand still, or die." As the artist got ready to defend himself, an escaped slave armed with an old musket stepped out from the high reeds. It was a close call at the hands of a desperate man. Kindly by nature, Audubon won his adversary's confidence, and found that the runaway and his wife and children had been separated at a slave auction, but had managed to escape into the wilderness, one by one, to attempt a wretched existence by hunting and fishing. Eventually, Audubon interceded with their latest owners, and had them restored to their original home through repurchase.

A British-born woman friend wrote of the Audubons as she knew them in Louisiana in the early 1820's, "Mrs. Audubon . . . had fine dark gray eyes, shaded by long dark lashes. Expression was her chief attraction. She was very gentle and intelligent. Her whole appearance impressed one with respect and admiration. Audubon was one of the handsomest men I ever saw . . . tall and slender, his blue eyes an eagle's in brightness. His bearing was courteous and refined, simple and unassuming. . . . He was a natural sportsman and artist . . . the center of attraction."

In 1824, the urgency of finding an engraver for his paintings and a publisher for his voluminous notes on bird life led Audubon to Philadelphia. There, he soon found himself welcomed by a notable group of scientists and artists. They included Thomas Sully, Dr. Richard Harlan, Thomas Say, and Titian and Rembrandt Peale. Audubon also met Edward Harris of Morristown, New Jersey, a wealthy landowner who was to become one of his staunchest, closest friends, a generous patron of his work, and his comrade nearly twenty years later on the last of his expeditions, up the Missouri River to the buffalo country of eastern Montana. Perhaps most important of all to Audubon's future was Charles Lucien Bonaparte, son of Napoleon's brother Lucien and even then, at twenty-one, a brilliant naturalist.

While the Philadelphia trip failed to produce an engraver for his work, Bonaparte crystallized the true ambition of Audubon's life by urging him to go to France or England and have his paintings of even the larger birds reproduced in accurate color and in actual life size. Audubon continued on to New York City, there to become a member of the Lyceum of Natural History, and to attract the attention of De Witt Clinton—one of New York's ablest Governors and an authority on the resources of the Empire State. At last Audubon had established himself as a naturalist and painter of the first rank in the minds of many influential men. Some of them were soon to assist him greatly in carrying out his vast undertaking.

Armed with introductory letters from Nolte, from Henry Clay's brother, John, and from many other prominent men in New Orleans, New York and Philadelphia, and burdened with a portfolio of more than two hundred bird paintings and drawings, Audubon set sail in 1826 on the 65-day voyage from New Orleans to Liverpool.

Within a week of his arrival in England the Rathbones, whom he met through Nolte's letter, arranged for an exhibition of Audubon's work at the Royal Institution in Liverpool. Within a single month he was famous. His pictures of the birds of America were the sensation of the intellectual world of England and Scotland—and their full-size reproduction now became a definite possibility.

The Liverpool triumph was soon followed by even greater success in an Edinburgh exhibition. No American had created such a furor abroad since Benjamin Franklin, about fifty years earlier. Audubon—even in Europe wearing the long hair and fringed buckskin jacket of an American woodsman—was entertained by men of title and culture, such as Lord Elgin, the Earl of Kinnoul, and Lord Stanley, fourteenth Earl of Derby, for whom the British horse-racing classic was named.

In Edinburgh, he took his first completed paintings to the engraver, W. H. Lizars, who made magnificent copper plates of a few of them, but soon had to stop the work because of strikes. There were moments now of deadly discouragement, and of loneliness and worry for Audubon. Writing from his room in Edinburgh late in 1826 to his wife, three thousand miles away in Louisiana, he

The final engraving in *The Birds of America* contains the fully elaborated versions of the birds Audubon sketched here—an evening grosbeak (left) and a fox sparrow (right)

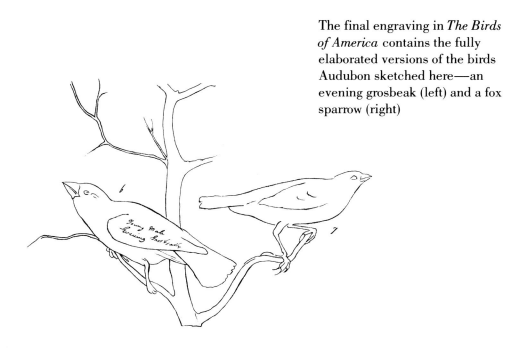

penned words that may find an echo today in many a man's mind: "Perhaps even yet, fame may be mine, and enable me to provide all that is needful for my Lucy and my children. Wealth I do not crave, but comfort. For my sons, I have the most ardent desire that they may receive the best of education, far above any that I possess. Day by day, science advances. New thoughts and new ideas crowd forward. There is always fresh food for enjoyment, study, improvement. I must place my boys where all this may be a possession to them."

The foremost scientists of Britain and the Continent became valuable advocates in securing subscriptions for *The Birds of America* from their own friends, and from their kings and the great museums and libraries. Audubon was awarded honorary membership in many of the most exclusive British literary, scientific, and art societies—a potent aid in creating demand for his portfolios.

Early in 1827 came the distinction he himself had coveted most of all—the opportunity to meet, in Scotland, the "Wizard of the North," Sir Walter Scott, then at the peak of his fame, whose motions at their first interview the artist "watched as I would those of a celestial being." Scott was impressed as well, for he wrote in his journal, "Audubon... less a Frenchman than I have ever seen, but great simplicity of manners... slight of person and plainly dressed, his countenance acute, handsome, and interesting... *His drawings are of the first order.*"

From Edinburgh, Audubon proceeded to London and Paris. He addressed the Royal Society in London, and read a paper exploding the ancient theory that vultures are attracted to carrion through their sense of smell, rather than by sight. Audubon recounted his own experiments in Louisiana in successfully luring vultures with odorless stuffed deerskins and exposed fresh carcasses, and his failure to attract them with concealed carrion, even in advanced stages of decay.

In London, Audubon met the Robert Havells, father and son, of a famous dynasty of English etchers and engravers. The son was then thirty-three. He would be forty-five before the gigantic work of printing *The Birds of America* was completed. He was more than a great engraver and a famous landscape painter in his own right, and for Audubon he was of long-term importance in many ways. His loyalty and serene temperament proved vital in encouraging the mercurial Audubon during the final, exhausting decade of his work in collecting and painting his birds.

Another London supporter of Audubon was Sir Thomas Lawrence, head of the Royal Academy and the most fashionable portrait painter to the British peerage and society. Sir Thomas helped Audubon out of at least one of his many acute financial crises. He made frequent visits to Audubon's squalid London lodgings, bringing with him wealthy patrons who paid high prices for Audubon's paintings of foxes, otters, and birds. But it was still a nip-and-tuck affair to keep creditors at bay.

France seemed to offer him a few green pastures, and he moved on to Paris. In the land of his boyhood, Audubon met one of the great naturalists of the century, Baron Cuvier, who described *The Birds of America* as "the most magnificent monument which has yet been raised to ornithology." In Paris, Audubon also gained the friendship of the Duke of Orléans and of Pierre Redouté, whose delicate floral paintings made him known as "the Rembrandt of the Roses." More to the point, France yielded thirteen new subscriptions.

In 1829 Audubon returned to America for a new round of collecting and painting additional species of birds, and to solicit American subscriptions which, at one thousand dollars the set, proved even harder to gather than among the aristocrats of the Old World. Soon, friendship brought him good fortune once more, in the assistance of Edward Everett of Massachusetts, whose abilities, displayed even in early manhood, made him for forty years one of the outstanding men in the United States—preacher, editor, professor, president of Harvard University, congressman, governor, U.S.

senator, foreign minister to Great Britain, and a public speaker of unrivaled power—until his old age, when Abraham Lincoln followed him on the dais at the Gettysburg cemetery. Everett was among Audubon's first American subscribers and most effective sponsors.

The year 1829 was a lively illustration of Audubon's industry. Arriving in New York in April from his first money-making European mission, he went first to Great Egg Harbor in southern New Jersey, to paint a wide variety of waterfowl, shorebirds, and waders. Then, by rail and wagon he penetrated the Great Pine Woods near Mauch Chunk, Pennsylvania, for thrushes, warblers, and finches, completing forty-two paintings of ninety-five different birds in less than four months.

In October, he made his way first to Louisville, then on to Bayou Sara in Louisiana for both the resident birds and the wintering migrants in the cypress swamps. A few months later, he was on his way back to England to raise funds to carry on his work. Subscribers became impatient over the slow pace of delivery of the successive new plates, but Audubon refused to debase his style for the sake of faster production. His painting was no simple snapshot technique. Every feather and scale was painstakingly drawn—Audubon spent over sixty hours in painting one eagle!

As if these exhausting activities were not enough, Audubon devoted thousands of hours, between 1827 and 1838, to another colossal project which had attracted him even earlier than the idea of painting *The Birds of America*. This was his *Ornithological Biography* which finally appeared as a five-volume series that runs to nearly three thousand pages. Cuvier pronounced it "the most gigantic book enterprise ever undertaken by a single individual."

Audubon's *Biography* contains scientific descriptions and hundreds of dramatic life histories of the bird species embraced in his paintings. It was sent as an informative supplement to subscribers for the plates. Based on Audubon's notes and journals covering a span of more than twenty years, the *Ornithological Biography* was edited by William MacGillivray, a young Scottish scientist whom Audubon met in Edinburgh, and whom he retained for this formidable literary undertaking for nearly nine years.

Leaf through the pages of the *Ornithological Biography* and the *Journals,* and thousands of instances of his wide-ranging observations leap into life. There, we see young woodpeckers whose tender beaks force them to dig only into soft, rotted stumps for grubs, while their elders can easily bore into the hard wood of living trees. Eagles hunt in pairs, to keep ducks diving until they are exhausted. Hawks use the same team technique to corner a flicker that would defy a single hawk, by circling around a trunk, out of reach. One species of flycatcher raises two broods in the long Pennsylvania summer, Audubon discovered, but only one brood in Canada. Juncos follow feeding grouse and wild turkeys for easy pickings of seeds and insects that their larger cousins scratch up from the earth. Indians in Arkansas hung gourds in their camps for purple martins to nest in, not by some tribal ritual, but because these big swallows drive away vultures, which would devour drying venison and tear pegged-out deer hides to tatters.

The perimeter of Audubon's observing eye was boundless. He could dissect a rattlesnake's fangs, or examine the plant parasite on a house fly, or learn why otters are found in greatest number near waterfalls. He watched a falcon in a treetop, bobbing her head in quick starts "as if counting each little space in the ground below." He wondered why a song sparrow builds three nests in a summer, one for each new brood, while a fish hawk returns every summer for a decade to the same eyrie. He noted that bobolinks fly northward in the spring by night, but move south by daylight in autumn, and that arctic sea birds dive to depths as great as ninety feet for food, only to be drowned in fish nets.

He studied the structure of the eyes of owls, trying to discover why subarctic species, accustomed to the midnight sun, see as clearly by day as at dusk, although some southern owls are so blind at noon that he saw one of them alight on the back of a cow, and lurch drunkenly off as the indignant animal bolted away. By his own notes and travels, he knew that swallows heading up from South America in the spring reach New Orleans in February, Louisville by mid-March, and St. Louis and Philadelphia only in the first days of April, and that kingfishers do not carry whole minnows to their nest-burrows until their young are half grown. These are a few random samples from five thick books.

Among the most strenuous of all of Audubon's expeditions was his Labrador journey, which lasted from early June into late August of 1833, when he was forty-eight years old, and brought to his brush scores of arctic gulls, ducks, falcons, sea birds, and grouse, rarely found farther south. His little schooner was often threatened by furious gales and unseen reefs, while Audubon worked eighteen hours a day to collect and paint birds. Then he would sit down to pen his notes, to express amazement that bank swallows flew about his fog-bound schooner in the face of an easterly gale—that a young Canada jay must have been incubated when temperatures were far below freezing—that eider ducks pluck down from their breasts to line their nests, without loosening their outer feathers—"like a woodsman clearing the undergrowth."

He would veer from the grandeur of an iceberg off Labrador "like a large man-of-war dressed in green muslin" to tell how fast the plants and young animals of that northern land mature in the long summer daylight. He would set down the depth and length of burrows where petrels and puffins nested, and report that seventeen men nearby butchered twenty-five hundred seals in three days.

Audubon saw the commercial eggers and feather hunters busy at their task, and wrote: "These people gather all the eider down they can find. They kill every bird that comes their way. So constant and persevering are their depredations that these species, exceedingly abundant twenty years ago, have abandoned their ancient breeding places. This war of extermination cannot last many years more. The eggers will be the first to repent the disappearance of the myriads of birds that made Labrador their summer residence."

Again, "We talked of the wild country around us and the enormous destruction of everything, except the rocks, which is going on here. The aborigines are melting away before a stronger race, as the wild animals are disappearing before them. Nature herself is perishing. Labrador must shortly be depopulated of every thing and every animal which has life and attracts the cupidity of men. When her fish, game, and birds are gone, she will be left alone, like a worn out field."

A man who sailed with Audubon to Labrador recalled him, sixty years later, in these revealing words: "When you had conversed with him for a moment, you looked on him as an old friend. To this day I can see him, a magnificent gray-haired man, childlike in his simplicity, kind-hearted, noble-souled, lover of Nature and of youth, friend of humanity, and one whose religion was the Golden Rule." Above all, Audubon himself was an individual, not a "common man."

He was proud of the opportunity America had given him to make his own way up from hunger and discouragement to world recognition and a considerable fortune. He had, in Dr. Brewer's words, "sacrificed everything that man holds dear—position in society, wealth, and every other ambition, to the one great aspiration that filled all his waking thoughts." His life was, indeed, an incredible sequence of adventures, hopes, disappointments, achievements, and the indomitable return, after every failure, to his fundamental task of completing the real mission of his existence—*The Birds of America* folios.

Audubon's sympathy for living beings was for him a matter of principle as well as feeling, and was put consistently into daily practice. Meeting a half-starved, barefoot child in the bitter cold of an Edinburgh December day, Audubon, close to rags himself, emptied the coppers from his pocket, and wrote in his *Journal*: "I never thought it necessary to be rich to help those poorer than we are. It is a duty to God, and to grow poorer in doing so is a blessing."

He recoiled in horror from a tour of a Liverpool prison and the barbarous brutality of the treadmill, to pour out his indignation at the idiocy of such torture as a corrective for petty crime, or a gain for society. Audubon's "heart ached" over the savage whipping a driver gave the coach horses to gain a lathered mile-an-hour on the Glasgow run. In London's Hyde Park, he bought a cage of Arctic finches from a sailor for no other purpose than to set them free at once. He could deny in his *Journal* that rum kills the Labrador Indian: "It is more often the want of food, the loss of hope as he loses sight of all that was abundant before the white man intruded on his land and killed off the wild animals."

Audubon was close to the profound social, economic and political turbulence that swept across the world—the overthrow of ancient kingdoms; the immigration of millions of hungry, oppressed people to America; the unrest that ushered in the Industrial Revolution; the recurrent speculative booms that lifted great numbers of Americans to swift prosperity; the depressions that crushed them into poverty as the human tide flooded westward; the battles between Andrew Jackson and the Federalists which cemented the foundations of our form of government.

Yet Audubon lived incredibly remote from all these conflicts and pressures. He left France just before the final struggles of Napoleon against England, Prussia, Austria, and Russia. He spent his mature life in the United States at a time when basic forces were setting the pattern of the century that followed his own time, and creating the world's strongest single industrial nation. He was not moved by these events. His consuming interest was in nature. His passion to watch and to paint birds, trees, flowers, and insects carried him far from civilization to tread trackless wilds where conflict and turbulence are the eternal facts of existence, as his prints starkly reveal.

New European and American travels still lay ahead in 1835, including a productive collecting trip from New Orleans along the Gulf Coast as far west as Galveston, early in 1837. By midsummer, Audubon was back in England. The most thrilling hour of his life must have come on a June day in 1838, when he stood with a little group of craftsmen in a London printing house, and saw the final plate completed, the last of the 435 big copper sheets from which *The Birds of America* was printed.

At least seventy-five sets of the *Birds* were originally sold to American individuals, museums, scientific groups, libraries and other subscribers. Some forty other sets were sold in France and Great Britain. A number of Audubon's foreign subscribers who received their sets, however, never paid for them. Among these were the Duchess of Clarence, the Marquis of Londonderry, the Princess of Hesse-Homburg, and King George IV of England! Baron Rothschild, one of the richest men in the world, subscribed but then refused to pay the modest price. Audubon remained abroad until the publication of the last volume of his *Ornithological Biography*, his "letterpress" on the American birds, in Edinburgh in 1839.

Then he came back to America for the last time, his spirit still eager for high adventure. He set out four years later at the age of fifty-eight, on an expedition up the Missouri to the mouth of the Yellowstone. Risking death at the hands of hostile Sioux and Assiniboines, he had one of his narrowest escapes when a wounded buffalo charged his horse, and missed a fatal crash by a yard.

That was perhaps the great artist's last threat from a living foe, after nearly six decades of facing hazards that had begun with the slave insurrections in Haiti in his infancy. He had brushed death many times at the fangs of diamondback rattlesnakes and cottonmouth moccasins in the southern swamps, by cholera and yellow fever in pestilential cities, by accident or the weapons of savage men in the wilderness, and by disaster at sea.

Audubon returned from the Missouri expedition to New York to help his sons work on their paintings of the *Quadrupeds of North America*. In 1841, he retired to his beautiful estate on the rural heights of upper Manhattan.

One of Audubon's friends during his later years was Samuel F. B. Morse—one of the foremost portrait painters of his time, and founder of the National Academy of Design—whose paintings of General Lafayette, President Monroe, De Witt Clinton, Henry Clay, and other eminent men are now displayed in New York City Hall, the Corcoran Art Gallery, and other collections.

In 1846, after his great invention, the telegraph, had been put into initial operation, Mr. Morse was a visitor at Audubon's home. In order to carry a telegraph line into New York City, Morse arranged for a wire to be strung high above the Hudson River from Fort Lee to his bedroom in Audubon's house, from which a relay line was laid to downtown Manhattan. Thus Audubon became a participant in the development of the telegraph. After an initial success, however, the experiment failed when the long wire, stretching in warm weather, sagged so low that it caught and was severed by the high mast of a ship on the Hudson. For several more years, Manhattan telegrams had to be sent by ferry between the New Jersey terminus and an office in Wall Street.

Among the prominent figures of his time whom Audubon could claim as his friends were four Presidents of the United States—Jackson, Van Buren, Harrison, and Tyler. There also were noted authors, such as Washington Irving and Jean Sismondi, and statesmen like Daniel Webster and

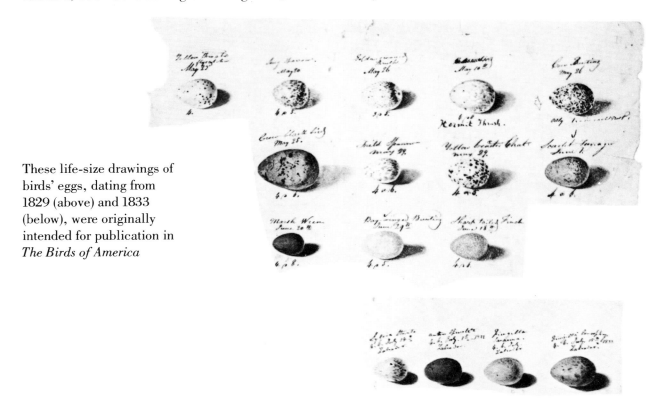

These life-size drawings of birds' eggs, dating from 1829 (above) and 1833 (below), were originally intended for publication in *The Birds of America*

Henry Clay. There were scientists of the stature of Charles Darwin, William MacGillivray, Dr. John Bachman, Thomas Nuttall, and Spencer Fullerton Baird.

There were men in the forefront of New England culture, too, such as Dr. George Parkman, Josiah Quincy, and Dr. George C. Shattuck. Other good friends of Audubon lived in a different setting—Daniel Boone, the river-boat captains on the Mississippi, the "wreckers" and turtle trappers of the Florida Keys, the Labrador sealers, the law-enforcing "regulators" of the western frontier, the Shawnee chief who slew bears with a knife, and other Indians with whom Audubon stalked wildfowl in the Tawapatee Bottoms in his early Kentucky days.

Friendships meant a great deal to Audubon, who spent many years in lonely wanderings in the American wilderness and as a foreigner traveling in distant lands. He despised quarrels and ignored slander. He once wrote: "I never can remember the name of an enemy. It is only my friends whom I remember."

In their various ways, *all* these men and scores of others in Audubon's life helped him toward the fulfillment of a mission that even he himself did not grasp until he was nearly forty years old. Without the tireless aid of many of them, he would never have reached his goal. Perhaps Audubon himself gratefully voiced the value of such friendships when he wrote: "Now a rambler in the wilds of America, glad to accept the hospitality of the humblest prairie squatter. Now the guest of a metropolitan aristocrat. Both gave freely, and he who, during the tough storms of life, can be in such spots has tasted happiness."

After Audubon's retirement, there were several sunset years of steady physical decline, ending on January 27, 1851, when at the age of sixty-six, he died in his home "like a child entering a beautiful sleep." His grave in Trinity Cemetery in upper Manhattan is marked by a large stone cross, carved with figures of the wild creatures he had known so well.

In his superb, definitive biography, *Audubon the Naturalist,* Francis Hobart Herrick observed: "... John James Audubon was one of those who, by a simple-hearted life of talent, devotion and enthusiasm, have freed themselves from the law of death. Audubon was a man of many sides, and his fame is due to a rare combination of those powers which were needed to accomplish the work that he finally set out to do. His personality was most winning, his individuality strong, and his long life, bent for the most part to attain definite ends, was checkered, adventurous and romantic beyond the common lot of men."

One of the finest tributes ever made to Audubon came after his death from a famous Scandinavian singer who, after a concert tour in the United States, had given generously to American charities. In return for one such donation, a New York protective fund sent her several valuable gifts, representative of this country. Her acknowledgment concluded with these words: "The splendid edition of Audubon's *Birds of America,* with which your resolution was accompanied, I shall always look upon as my most beautiful souvenir of America." The note was written by a woman whose own glorious voice joined her to the great company of the songbirds—for all the world knows her as the "Swedish Nightingale," Jenny Lind.

Audubon left to his adopted country the heritage of his art and writings. The plates for *The Birds of America* were destroyed by fire in 1845, but nearly all the original paintings from which they were made are in the possession of the New-York Historical Society. He also left to us the inspiration to fight to preserve the American wilderness, whose destruction he foresaw in the human sea of settlement flooding westward more than a century ago. As one of Audubon's early biographers, General James Grant Wilson, wrote in 1869: "While the melody of the mockingbird is heard in the cypress swamps of Louisiana, or the shrill scream of the eagle on the frozen shores of the northern seas, the name of John James Audubon will live in the hearts of his grateful countrymen."

Today, Audubon is regarded as the patron saint of American wildlife conservation—and properly so, even though he was obliged to use his own gun unsparingly to secure perfect specimens for his work. It was not unusual for him to shoot a hundred birds in a day, and his small collecting party killed several hundred birds, of 104 different species, in just a few days in 1837, along the Louisiana coast! His toll was light, however, against the value of his work and the beauty which his paintings have brought to millions of homes throughout the world.

Audubon had a more practical grasp of conservation than was widely held in his time—or is, even in our own. The economic status of the common crow, for example, is still a highly controversial topic of farmers and sportsmen. Audubon pointed out long ago that crows unquestionably devour the eggs of gamebirds and songbirds, kill young or weakened animals that fall in their path, and pull up seed and sprouting grain. Yet he said: "I endeavor to speak of the crow with all due impartiality, not wishing to conceal its faults nor its merits. I can well assure the farmer that if it were not for the crow, thousands of cornstalks would every year fall prostrate, being cut over close to the ground by the destructive grubs called cut-worms."

Yet today, while crows and several other species are being shot on sight in many parts of the country as enemies of mankind, biologists disclose that a crow's stomach contained 200 crop-destroying caterpillars; a plover's, 300 mosquito larvae; a hawk's, 340 grasshoppers; and an owl's fur pellets, more than a dozen field mice.

As early as his first trip to Great Britain in 1826, Audubon recognized the perils which even then threatened the scenic beauty, the wild animals, and the very soil and water of North America. Being also a great admirer of Sir Walter Scott, Audubon wrote in his *Journal* in December, 1826, in Edinburgh: "How many times have I longed for Sir Walter Scott to come to my beloved country that he might describe, as no one else ever can, the stream, the swamp, the river, the mountain, for the sake of future ages. A century hence they will not be there as I see them. Nature will have been robbed of many brilliant charms. The rivers will be tormented and turned from their primitive courses, the hills will be leveled with the swamps and perhaps the swamp will have become a mound, surmounted by a fortress of a thousand guns. The deer may exist nowhere, fish will no longer abound in the rivers, the eagle scarce ever alight, and the millions of lovely songsters be driven away or slain by man. Without Sir Walter Scott, these beauties must perish, unknown to the world." But it was Audubon, and not Scott, whose pen and paint have made these beauties imperishable!

Watching the wasteful, senseless butchery of the buffalo on the western plains in 1843, Audubon said: "This cannot last. Even now there is a perceptible difference in the size of the herds. Before many years the buffalo, like the great auk, will have disappeared." In the ensuing two decades, over sixty-eight million buffalo were slaughtered under the smashing impact of white men intent upon the winning of the West. By 1890, those animals were nearly exterminated.

It is possible that animals like the buffalo, the Carolina parakeet, and the passenger pigeon could not have survived in anything like their original way of life under any practical form of protection. The vast, uncontrollable herds of migratory buffalo could not be allowed to remain at large on a continent spanned by fences, railroads, wheat ranches, and truck caravans. The billions of wild pigeons that depended on mass association over our ancient, endless oak and beech forests could not adjust their feeding habits to a land of contoured farms and scattered woodlots.

Many alert minds have explored the reasons for the survival or extinction of various animals. Darwin, over a hundred years ago, pointed out that no continental species succumbs abruptly throughout a large area. It becomes scarce, then rare, and finally extinct in one region, and then in another, before it vanishes forever from the roll call of the world's living creatures.

Far more precarious is the existence of island birds, easy prey to imported animals and to the competition of imported birds, and with no way to escape. This was illustrated by the swift disappearance of many beautiful native birds from Hawaii and Puerto Rico after the importation of the mongoose.

Darwin noted, too, that "if we ask why this or that species is rare, we can answer that something is unfavorable in its conditions of life, but what that something is, we can hardly ever tell." That is why modern conservationists, when any animal decreases in numbers for a prolonged period, try to ascertain the unfavorable conditions that may surround it and ask for special protective measures that may help it to stage a sound recovery. This policy has often been successful, as in the case of the wood duck, the most beautiful of American waterfowl.

Most challenging, in human no less than in wildlife affairs, was Darwin's unrefuted statement that the deadliest warfare on this planet is not waged between a bird and the worm or insect it kills, nor between a hawk and the sparrow it catches, but among creatures of the same or allied species. This conflict stems from the savage competition for a limited supply of food, cover, water, and breeding territory. In that eternal strife, only the fittest can survive. The weak, aging, or defective individuals are obviously the most vulnerable to death by natural causes, whether by disease, drought, storm, the fangs of the fox, or the way of the eagle.

Man, however, is not nearly so selective in his killing, and has sometimes been unwise in his well-meant interference with wildlife. He has many times broken the delicate, complex chain of natural events to his own cost, and brought doom to entire species and the threat of extinction to others. When the Kaibab mule deer in Arizona were "protected" by killing off the mountain lions and coyotes that preyed upon them, the herd grew from four thousand to one hundred thousand in twenty years. The deer then devoured their browse and even stripped away the thin topsoil over large areas, and sixty thousand of them starved to death in two winters.

The pendulum of public opinion toward conservation—"wise use for the proper purpose at the right time"—has swung far since Audubon's time, but wildlife conservation still has a long distance to travel in public comprehension and political action before its potentialities can be realized in higher general living standards and greater security. The dramatic first step in stirring America to the urgency of saving wild animals and birds was to arouse us to their interest, human usefulness, and beauty. That was the achievement of Audubon and of thousands of naturalists, artists, and conservationists who have followed him.

The second stride is the hard process of educating oncoming generations to the interdependence of men and the land and its other living inhabitants—from soil bacteria to songbirds and spruce trees—from earthworms to falcons and grasslands—from bees to coyotes and woodpeckers—from field mice to bluebirds and rainbow trout. When man weakens or breaks a link in the complex food chains of the wilderness, he pays the cost in cash.

We have outlived the day when Audubon saw tons of robins for sale in the New Orleans market. Yet we may go to the other extreme and overlook the mathematics that allows a single pair of robins and their successive broods, if unchecked by natural forces, to build a self-starving horde of over 671 million robins in less than fifteen years. In our concern to protect the wildlife we most enjoy, we cannot afford to exterminate it by blindly destroying the predatory controls that keep these animal populations—for their welfare and our own—adjusted to the capacity of their food supply and hunting space.

Today's critical problems of conservation are far broader than the protection of this or that species of animal. They are rooted in the difficulty of preserving extensive areas of the wilderness itself. The world's human population is soaring even now at an astronomical rate. The remaining land, water, forests, minerals, and many other natural resources of the globe are growing more and more vital to mankind's own survival in any tolerable way of living.

The stature of Audubon as a prophet grows greater against the fateful drama, as we look back upon the wonders of nature which he knew so well and which his paintings preserved for later generations. There are few homes in America where the spirit of Audubon is not cherished now as an example for our children to follow in safeguarding the beauty of the land he had made his own.

Today, Audubon's name is a byword for the sound conservation of our wildlife, no less than for one of the world's great naturalists and watercolor artists.

Audubon once remarked in his *Journal*: "I know that I am a poor writer. I can scarcely manage to scribble a tolerable English letter, and not a much better one in French. I know that I am not a scholar. But I am also aware that no other man living knows better than I do the habits of our birds. No man living has studied them as I have done. I can at least set down plain truths about them, which may be useful and even interesting."

In writing to his close friend and collaborator, the Reverend John Bachman, in 1835, when Audubon was fifty years old, he said, "What a treat for me to disclose things unknown to all the world until now! Assist me all you can. Enable me to publish no trash, nothing but facts. My work will be a standard one for ages to come. Except for some few errors, the truths contained in my writings and paintings will become ever more apparent. I am growing old fast, and must work at double-quick time to assure completion of my work."

Audubon's work was triumphantly completed after more than thirty years of hard work, against all the obstacles of early poverty, perilous travel in a pioneer land, and the solitude of long separations from the family he loved. The truths that he set down are cherished by millions of Americans. As long as our civilization lasts, the world will owe a debt to John James Audubon for his supreme lifework, the painting of *The Birds of America* and the writing of the *Ornithological Biography*.

EDITOR'S NOTE: The commentaries in the following section, "Thirty Great Audubon Birds," are illustrated with colorplates engraved by Robert Havell for the Elephant Folio edition of *The Birds of America* (1827–1838). The catalogue that follows the commentaries is a complete enumeration of the five hundred plates appearing in the 1871 edition, lithographed by J. T. Bowen of Philadelphia. The Bowen plates are reproduced courtesy of the Library of Congress, Washington, D.C.

# Thirty
# Great Audubon Birds

# 1

# Blue-winged Teal

*(Anas discors)*
ABOVE: female; BELOW: male*

ONE OF THE SMALLER fresh-water ducks, this is strictly a New World species. The blue-winged teal migrates in early autumn and early to mid-spring, with one of the longest yearly travel spans of any American waterfowl. It breeds from the Atlantic to the Pacific coasts, but the main distributional center is in our central and western prairie grassland marshes, ponds, and potholes and far into north-western Canada. Recent research even suggests that it is a regular breeder in locally specific areas of Alaska. The vast majority of blue-winged teals winter south of the United States, primarily along the Gulf Coast through Mexico, but even down to central Chile and the vicinity of Buenos Aires, Argentina. One of the most amazing flight records established by any of the millions of birds so far banded under the United States Fish and Wildlife Service was made by a blue-winged teal. This duck, banded in Quebec on September 5, 1930, was shot twenty-eight days later in Guyana. As the airline distance is 2,400 miles, this teal displayed an average cruising speed of at least 85 miles a day.

These dainty little ducks fly and feed in close-bunched flocks, thus exposing themselves to heavy shooting loss. Audubon once saw ninety-four blue-winged teals brought down by a hunter with two shots. More menacing than the hunting toll for the survival of these birds, however, is the destruction, by drainage or "development," of the native grass-land areas and associated sloughs and marshes and of the true and tall-grass prairies so vital as their breeding habitat.

This species lays from six to eleven eggs on average in a basket-like nest on dry sites, usually within a quarter-mile of water. A race of the blue-winged teal occurs west of the Rocky Mountains, but is outnumbered there by the cinnamon teal, to which it is closely related. The blue-winged's small size and rapid wing beat had long credited it with tremendous flight speeds, and although it is a strong flier, recent plane checks show that its actual air velocity seldom exceeds 50 miles an hour, somewhat slower than the canvasbacks and a few other large wildfowl. Teal are sometimes overtaken by falcons, but often manage to escape by adroit maneuvers.

*The heading of each commentary contains the following information: the modern name of the bird; its Latin designation; the name Audubon gave it in his *Ornithological Biography*, if that differs from the modern name; and identifications of sexes and plant life, when these are given on the Havell plate.

# 2

# Band-tailed Pigeon

*(Columba fasciata)*
ABOVE: female; BELOW: male
PLANT: *Cornus nuttalli*

IN 1837, TOWARD the close of his thirty-year task of painting the *Birds of America*, Audubon was sent a few skins of a strange wild dove from the Pacific Coast. They were band-tailed pigeons, which in size, flight pattern, and habits resemble domestic pigeons. The artist never saw these magnificent birds in the wilderness, but he was given accurate information about them by the scientist-collector of his models, Dr. John K. Townsend, who observed thousands of band-taileds on his expedition to the Columbia River in 1834–37. These pigeons lay only one egg to the nest, and breed usually only once — sometimes twice—a year, the lowest reproductive rate of any North American game bird except the extinct passenger pigeon. In California, there are records of up to three broods per season reared.

The abundance of these birds fluctuates widely, depending on food supply and hunting pressures. During the latter part of the nineteenth century, more than half their entire population succumbed to hunters in Santa Barbara County, California. The abundant local crop of acorns and the scarcity of food elsewhere brought tens of thousands of band-tailed pigeons to this region, which was also accessible to great numbers of sportsmen. The slaughter led to studies on the reproductive biology of the pigeon and subsequently to protective laws, which gradually restored the birds to abundance. Later, heavy depredations by these pigeons upon farm crops called for larger gamebags; the surplus pigeons were decimated in seasons of acute shortage of wild nuts, seeds, and buds, or of exceptionally high pigeon population.

Band-tailed pigeons require large forested areas or heavily wooded canyon slopes in which to nest. They breed from the middle of western British Columbia southward into Baja California and in mountain forests from central Utah and northern Colorado southward into Costa Rica and Panama. A few of these birds winter as far north as Puget Sound, while most others move south in autumn to California, central Arizona, west Texas, and New Mexico, returning north in April. The lone squab is fed three or four times daily, even when first hatched, and its rations are reduced to a single meal a day before it leaves its oftentimes frail and flimsy nest. Flocks in winter usually number from ten to forty birds, but thousands may gather at a mineral-water hole or at a salt spring for dietary reasons that are unclear to biologists. In summer band-taileds are scattered in small numbers over vast wooded regions from the eastern Rockies to the Cascade and Coast ranges, but they avoid the intervening High Sierras, and are rarely seen far from timberlands.

# 3

# *Arctic Tern*

*(Sterna paradisaea)*

No OTHER BIRD has won so wide a reputation for its globe-trotting travel routes as this graceful little seabird. There are spectacular recoveries of banded Arctic terns which demonstrate that it can fly almost the whole length of the world twice each year, between its breeding grounds and its winter haunts. Thus, it spends more of its life in daylight than any other species, in the two lands of the midnight sun. The Arctic tern nests up to within 700 miles of the North Pole, in Canada, Greenland, Europe, and Siberia. In the northern autumn, it flies south as far as the stormy seas off the Antarctic ice-shelf. The round trip distance is about 22,000 miles, not counting such sidewise cruising as is required by the thousands of these terns that travel eastward from North America to the coast of France before heading south off the western shores of Spain and Africa. This species is seldom seen south of Long Island on our Atlantic seaboard, although many of them breed on islands off the Maine coast.

The Arctic tern so closely resembles the common tern of the middle and tropical latitudes of the Old World and the New that separation of adults of these species can be based only on the Arctic's relatively shorter legs, noticeably so when the bird perches; shorter, finer bill; all dark-red bill color; small, rounded head, grayer underparts, and deeply forked tail with longer tail streamers; and definite thin trailing edge of black on the very outer edges of the wings. Admittedly these distinctions require ideal viewing at close range to be usable. Both of these terns have the same feeding customs—with down-pointed beak and beating their wings in a swift overhand rowing motion, they cruise as buoyantly as butterflies over the surf and the ocean, turn or twist suddenly, hover or skim low over a school of small fish, and then dive into the water. Usually they emerge quickly, and fly back to shore with a tiny fish or crustacean held crosswise in their sharp beaks. They prefer to nest in a scrape in sand or moss, where their eggs and spotted, downy chicks are hard to find among the pebbles and broken seashells.

Terns usually nest in colonies and are quick to attack human and other intruders in mass formations, diving bravely and often inflicting bloody scalp wounds. Their eggs and young are vulnerable to cats, raccoons, rats, gulls, and crows. Arctic terns are noisy creatures, uttering a long sharp "tee-arrr" alarm cry and a variety of staccato snarls and chuckles. The male bird often comes to his incubating mate to bring her a fish—a procedure that also plays a part in their courtship behavior. Audubon's painting was made on his perilous Labrador expedition in 1833.

# 4

# Wild Turkey Gobbler

*(Meleagris gallopavo)*
Male

AUDUBON'S SUPERB PLATE of the wild turkey gobbler is the most famous of all the 435 prints of his Elephant Folio. It is also first in that series and the most valuable to collectors. A full-sized (25 x 38″), first-edition print with full margins, in excellent condition, recently commanded the handsome sum of $12,000. The picture was painted in West Feliciana Parish in central Louisiana in 1825 and was modeled after a bird that the artist had shot in Sleepy Hollow Woods, one of his favorite hunting areas. This print is noteworthy for another reason. In 1827 the wife of one of Audubon's wealthy British sponsors had a Liverpool engraver design from this print a wild turkey signet ring as her personal gift to the artist. Under the miniature of the gobbler was Audubon's own motto, "America My Country," significant of the gratitude and devotion of a French immigrant toward his adopted land.

Probably the finest game birds in the world, these huge bronze-colored creatures are not only swift of wing but also fleet of foot and have been clocked while running at 15 miles per hour. The gobblers (males) are much larger and more deeply bronze-colored than the hens, and Audubon saw one bird that reportedly weighed thirty-six pounds and wore a beard a foot long. In the mating season, gobblers make their elaborate strutting displays much like peacocks, spreading their tails fanwise, and are known to stage impressive combats for harems of hens, striking at their opponent's head with beak, spurs, and wings. A male, by strutting and calling, usually attracts a harem averaging five or six females, with a rare twelve to fourteen being known. Like the quail and grouse, wild turkeys spend most of their time on the ground in search of food, but in the evening they almost always roost in trees. They provide a supreme table delicacy when they have fed on their usual wilderness fare of acorns, fruit, berries, grasses, and seeds.

# 5

# Screech Owl

*(Otus asio)*
"Little Screech Owl"
PLANT: Jersey Pine. *Pinus inops*

MORE WIDELY KNOWN by its soft, mellow, quavering trill than by sight, the misnamed "screech" owl is among the most abundant of the nocturnal birds of prey throughout most of the United States and southward to central Mexico. Small in size, droll in appearance, and accustomed to human haunts, this highly efficient "flying mousetrap" is a frequent occupant of orchards, the borders of suburban woodlands, and even city parks. It seldom hunts before darkest night, remaining concealed by day even to people who move close to its roosting place in a dense evergreen, an old woodpecker hole, or a hollow tree. Occasionally in the spring, however, parent screech owls become extremely audacious twilight assailants, flying at the faces of passersby who innocently walk near the nest or beneath a fledgling owlet. The eighteen subspecies of screech owl in North America vary greatly in size, coloration, and hunting customs, from the large, pale eastern subspecies (*Otus asio naevius*) to its dark, small Florida cousin (*Otus asio floridanus*) and the light-colored, handsome Rocky Mountain (*Otus asio maxwelliae*) and Northwest Coast screech owls (*Otus asio kennicottii*).

An interesting feature of this owl species, shared by a few other birds, is that it is markedly dichromatic, that is, it has two distinct color phases—one of them red, the other gray—as shown in Audubon's plate. The color phases are haphazardly random and are not related to the bird's sex or age, nor to the season. Broods containing nestlings of one or both colors may occur regardless of whether the parents are of one or both phases. Screech owls feed primarily on insects, but during the winter they will eat noninsect food: mice, young rabbits and rats, frogs, crayfish, and, to some extent, small birds. In turn, screech owls are a favorite quarry for larger owls, most frequently the great horned owl. They are also actively harassed by jays, crows, or magpies when discovered by day in an exposed spot.

Screech owls nest in hollow branches or trunks, usually laying four to six eggs. Their heavy toll of injurious rodents and insects has given screech owls strict legal protection in most states. These comical-looking little owls do not migrate, but may range considerable distances seasonally under pressure of local food shortages, especially in years when the "boom-and-crash" cycle of the field mouse population, over any large area, has reached a low ebb.

# 6

# Great Blue Heron

*(Ardea herodias)*
Male

STANDING FOUR FEET high with its head raised, this splendid bird is outranked in size, among our wading birds, only by the cranes and by the great white heron of extreme southern Florida, which is now considered merely a subspecies of the great blue heron. Its summer range extends from southeastern Alaska to Nova Scotia and southward to Mexico and the West Indies, while in winter it generally withdraws from the North to ice-free lowlands. With its lancelike beak, the great blue heron is an excellent "spear-gunner" in pursuit of minnows, suckers, and other small, nongame fish, and of mice, young rats, frogs, and insects. It has even been seen deftly seizing butterflies on the wing. Describing its hunting procedure, Audubon wrote: "How grand is the scene! The tread of the tall bird no one hears, so carefully does he place his foot on the moist ground. Now his golden eye glances over the surroundings, taking advantage of the full stretch of his graceful neck. He lays his head on his shoulders...a statue of a bird, so motionless he is. Now he has taken a silent step, slowly he raises his head and now, what a sudden start! His formidable bill has transfixed a

perch, which he beats to death on the ground. With difficulty, he gulps it down. His broad wings open, and away he slowly flies to another station."

The great blue heron is impressive in flight, its long legs trailing straight back, its neck S-curved so that the nape rests on its back, the wings with a six-foot span oaring steadily in slow beats. The adult birds are mainly solitary and wary and become gregarious only in the nesting season, gathering in heronries with oftentimes more than fifteen nests in a single high tree. The courtship duels of the male birds display a skill in thrust-and-parry worthy of D'Artagnan. From three to five eggs (usually four) are laid, and both parents take part in feeding their squealing, ravenous young, which, like the eggs, are under considerable threat from crows, gulls, hawks, and owls. This heron usually impales a fish crosswise, then tosses it into the air, catches and swallows it headfirst. A wounded great blue heron is dangerous to approach, its rapier beak stabbing with lightning speed at the eyes of any man or dog venturing within range.

# 7.

# Passenger Pigeon

*(Ectopistes migratorius)*
ABOVE: female; BELOW: male

"THE ROAR OF THEIR wings was like a tornado in the treetops, and the morning was darkened as by a heavy thunder shower," wrote an observer of the countless passenger pigeons that nested in northern Pennsylvania as recently as 1870. Yet on September 1, 1914, "Martha," the last surviving specimen of this magnificent bird—"the finest pigeon the world has seen"—died a captive in the Cincinnati Zoological Gardens. From the early explorations of Canada by Cartier and Champlain, down through the first half of the nineteenth century, hundreds of men recorded the astounding hosts of billions of passenger pigeons that moved in dense, multilayered, sky-darkening flocks over North America, from Florida and west Texas to northern Manitoba and Nova Scotia, guided by the seasons and the fluctuating food supply. Audubon calculated that a single three-hour flight of pigeons he observed in Kentucky numbered more than a billion birds, and that this was only a small part of a three-day movement! As late as 1882, in six weeks from Milwaukee alone, nearly two million pigeons were delivered in cold storage to eastern markets. But, in 1909, rewards were posted from coast to coast for the discovery of even a single, living wild pigeon, and no one has yet come forward to claim them!

The passenger pigeon was about the size of a domestic pigeon in bulk, but its longer, sharply pointed tail gave it a length of fifteen to eighteen inches. The deep blue-gray on the head and back and the black tail plumage, along with the richly iridescent gold and violet of the neck, made the male passenger pigeon more colorful than the smaller mourning dove, which is still abundant over most of our continent. The fate of the passenger pigeon was sealed by four principal factors: merciless, wholesale exploitation for the market by man, the primary factor; a low breeding rate and a low reproductive potential—only one nesting a year and only one, rarely two, eggs to the nest; many of the natural decimating forces, such as weather, disease, predators, and the perils of migration; and finally, and least in importance, the inability of these regal birds to adapt themselves biologically to small breeding and roosting groups.

Such was the tragic destiny of a species that, at its peak of population, is believed to have constituted between twenty-five and forty percent of the billions of birds inhabiting colonial North America. However, the extermination of the passenger pigeon did arouse the public to the impending doom threatening several other beautiful and valuable birds, and led to protective measures that saved them from the game hog and the market and plumage hunter.

# 8

# *Blue Jay*

*(Cyanocitta cristata)*
ABOVE: female; BELOW, LEFT: female; BELOW, RIGHT: male

AMONG THE WARIEST, most intelligent, and most brilliantly colored year-round residents of the eastern and midwestern states, west to the Rockies, and of southern Canada, the blue jay is also one of our more economically valuable species, in spite of its tarnished reputation. Audubon's plate itself presents probably the most prejudicial view of this jay, with its propensity for robbing the nests of some smaller birds. However, egg-eating can be charged against the blue jay only during the few short weeks of the nesting season each summer; because the damage is minimal, the survival of no species is menaced. For the rest of the year, its feeding preferences are either harmless or highly beneficial to man, consisting partly of small reptiles, mice, grasshoppers, tent caterpillars, fruit-destroying beetles, acorns, beechnuts, corn, and weed seeds. At all seasons, this jay is one of our most vociferous birds as well as an adept mimic, with a wide vocal repertory of loud screams, chatters, and alarm cries mixed with soft warblings and faithful imitations of the notes of many other birds, including hawks, wrens, flycatchers, sparrows, and catbirds.

Blue jays are self-appointed guardians of the wilderness. They gather swiftly in noisy groups to mob, harass, and drive into hiding cats, foxes, owls, and other predatory creatures detected in the open. They are equally quick to sound the alarm and assembly calls when hunters and other human intruders venture into the wilderness, although in towns and farming country they are unafraid of man. They come readily to feeding stations, and individual jays have even been taught to fly to the hands or shoulders of suburban bird lovers for sunflower seeds.

A considerable number of blue jays remain far north through even the most severe winters, but the majority of the northern birds fly a few hundred miles southward in autumn, some as far south as the Carolinas. Those that nest in our more temperate regions probably remain there throughout the year, judging by hundreds of records of banded birds. In years of acute food scarcity in the North, the irregular southward movement may develop into a mass invasion of the middle states by jays from Canada and the border states, with hundreds of them flying past an observer in a few hours of an October day.

# 9

# Gyrfalcon

*(Falco rusticolus)*
"Iceland or Jer Falcon"
Females

LARGEST OF THE WORLD'S falcons, the gyr ranks among the power-diving champions of the sky, reaching a velocity close to 200 miles an hour in a death-dealing, near-vertical stoop on its quarry, from a height of half a mile. It is a creature of the high Arctic, rarely seen even in our northern states. With its four-foot wingspread, great speed, and accurate talons, the gyrfalcon is a formidable and efficient hunter of lemmings, hares, waterfowl, grouse, ptarmigan, and sea birds. This falcon also commonly hunts by flying fast near the ground and catching its prey directly once on the wing. Its color variations run from dark gray-brown through pale gray to almost pure white. Dark birds are generally found only in the southerly parts of the range, in the low Arctic regions, while the gray phase and almost pure white phase occur mainly in the high Arctic. The Audubon plate shown here was painted from a captive Iceland gyrfalcon, for in his own travels in the subarctic, Audubon saw and collected only the dark race found in Labrador.

In the Middle Ages, white gyrfalcons were prized far above all other hawks for the much-pursued sport of falconry and were reserved exclusively for emperors and kings. During one of the Crusades, the Duke of Nevers was ransomed by the Saracen leader Saladin for the price of only a few of these splendid dark-eyed, snowy falcons. Falconry, the training and use of birds of prey for the pursuit of game and personal entertainment, has been practiced in Asia, the Near East, and North Africa for thousands of years by those with sufficient open country and ample leisure time. It spread from the East to civilized Europe and from there to Australia and to North America. Today, this "sport of kings" is still actively followed east of Suez. Hawks and falcons trapped in the Syrian desert and the Indian plains are regularly offered for sale in the bazaars of Damascus and Benares. In the western world this archaic sport has struggled to survive against the drastic decline in the past century in numbers of wild hawks, abundance of game, and areas of open hunting country in Europe, Britain, and the New World.

Unlike the other principal members of the falcon clan in North America, the gyrfalcon does not have to run a deadly gauntlet of shot and shell from hunters in the United States and has few natural enemies in its normal, northern range. Its numbers are limited only by its characteristic of not breeding every year (it appears to breed in alternate years) and by cyclical fluctuations in the ptarmigan population. Both breeding frequency and breeding success seem closely affected by winter starvation of the adults and food availability during breeding season.

# 10

# Black-billed Magpie

*(Pica pica)*
"Common Magpie"
ABOVE: male; BELOW: female

ALTHOUGH IT IS identical with the black-billed magpie of Great Britain, northern Europe, and Asia, the American black-billed magpie, as Audubon himself noted, is strangely absent from eastern North America. Yet it is abundant in suitable territory westward from Kansas and the Dakotas to California and coastal Alaska. A flashy, garrulous member of the family *Corvidae,* the magpie has striking white and iridescent velvety-black plumage and a grotesquely long tail, glossy, greenish-blue, and wedge-shaped. It is thus one of the more spectacular large birds of the willow-lined watercourses, upland pastures, and sagebrush open spaces of the West. Even in the nesting season, magpies enjoy the company of others of their kind. They usually are seen in loose flocks, numbering up to a few dozen birds, but never in the huge swarms into which crows assemble to roost and feed in autumn and winter. Like other members of their tribe, magpies are omnivorous. They feed on grain and fruit, trapped or crippled animals, the eggs and young of other birds, rodents, carrion, reptiles, insects, shellfish, and any provender they can steal from campsites or other human habitations.

During the wars with the Plains Indians, hungry magpies were a constant winter plague, attacking the cavalrymen's wounded or saddlesore mounts. In captivity, these bold, handsome birds readily pick up snatches of human speech; in the wilderness their unceasing jargon shifts from the wooden, rattling chatter of their primary alarm call to guttural bleats, crooning appeals, explosive snorting, warbling subsong, and comical croaks. Their flight is not heavy and labored, as one might suspect, although the short wings sometimes appear to encounter a drag in towing the "trailer-van" tail. They seldom rise high in the air, and seek their food mainly by stalking sedately about on the ground, with occasional abrupt leaps and zigzag flutterings. However, the speed they can muster when flying up and the agility they exhibit when dodging predators are legendary. Magpies delight in harassing any owl, cat, or fox they surprise by daylight, and with raucous battle cries hover above it in gangs. The magpie's nest is a bulky, domed pile of sticks, with an opening on each side leading to a well-lined, cuplike cradle, in which from two to eight (usually five to seven) eggs are laid. Undoubtedly this type of nest greatly discourages predators and has been an important factor in the success and expansion of the magpie.

Because of their predatory ways, magpies have been relentlessly hunted for centuries by hunters and game wardens in Great Britain and Europe, and by farmers and sportsmen in North America since the days of the earliest settlers. Yet they occupy a useful place in the delicate chain of nature, both by acting as scavengers and by helping to reduce the surplus population of insects and rodents in the copious reproduction cycles of the wilderness.

# 11

# Louisiana Heron

*(Hydranassa tricolor)*
Adult male

MORE ACCURATELY DESCRIBED by its Greek and Latin scientific title of "red-necked, tricolored water queen," this slenderest of our many herons, and one of the swiftest of flight, occupies a far vaster range than within the borders of the Pelican State. Its nesting territory extends down from Massachusetts to Florida and the Gulf States, westward to Baja California, and as far beyond our own boundary as northwestern Ecuador, the West Indies, and northeastern Brazil. Its winter habitat stretches from the Gulf States well into South America. The Louisiana heron is the most abundant of all its tribe in the coastal marshes and cypress swamps of the South. It was of this creature that Audubon wrote: "Delicate in form, beautiful in plumage, graceful in movement, I never see this interesting heron without calling it 'Lady of the Waters.'" By day, these dignified birds are almost constantly on the hunt, flying from one feeding haunt to another and stalking their prey, in shallow water or on land, by stealthy, silent advances and brief, watchful pauses before the stab of the sharp beak impales a victim. Their food consists mainly of frogs, killifish, minnows, shrimp, crayfish, mice, and insects.

At the conclusion of the nesting season in midsummer, a few Louisiana herons, along with many egrets, herons, and other waders, travel far westward and northward on wanderings that may take them as far as Nova Scotia, Wisconsin, and Colorado. It has not yet been determined whether such extensive meanderings are a means by which nature breaks up the family and colonial groups, an escape from a depleted food supply, or the result of some other cause. Some biologists theorize that these movements are correlated with the development of the gonads in young birds and that unfavorable weather conditions in the North reverse the trend of the gonads and the travel direction.

In adult plumage Louisiana herons are not likely to be confused with any other heron. The mature bird has a crested, slaty head, nape, and back; a white rump and belly; whitish throat stripe; white and purple head and neck plumes; and rather cinnamon-colored back plumes. The little blue heron, which is slightly smaller, is pure white, with gray wing tips, in its juvenal plumage. As an adult, it displays a purplish head and neck and has a solidly lead-colored body and underparts. Louisiana herons customarily nest in colonies, between March and June. Before they are able to fly, the young birds—which are decidedly redder than the adults—learn to scramble about in the trees and mangrove thickets and buttonwood islands, using their beaks, wings, and feet adroitly to keep from falling into the perilous water below, where large fish or reptiles of many species would be quick to seize them.

# 12

# Florida Scrub Jay

*(Aphelocoma coerulescens coerulescens)*
"Florida Jay"
ABOVE: females; BELOW: male
PLANT: Persimmon Tree. *Diospyros virginiana*

THIS SLIM, COLORFUL jay is a dweller of the scrub oak of Florida, which is characterized by low, dense thickets containing numerous open sandy spaces. It is monogamous and sedentary, and demonstrates an interesting biological social characteristic: cooperative breeding, that is, individuals other than the parent birds assist in the care of the young, territorial defense, and nest defense. The majority of these "helpers" are nonbreeding, one- or two-year-old birds that are offspring of the pair they are assisting. These "helpers" leave their parents' territory at maturity—when they are approximately two years old—then pair with unrelated birds, establishing new territories in thickets dominated by oak species, where individual trees are usually less than ten feet in height. With its large, deep-powder-blue head, dull gray-blue cheek patches, royal-blue wings and rump, and long, strongly graduated tail, the colorful, uncrested Florida scrub jay cannot be mistaken for the familiar eastern blue jay or the much darker blue, crested jays of the West. The alarm call of this jay is harsh and grating, and its other cries closely resemble the notes of the large boat-tailed grackle.

Although tolerant of mankind and still fairly common in the midwestern part of the state, the Florida jay is steadily yielding ground to the clearing of its scrub haunts, and is no longer found in many parts of the peninsula where it was once abundant. Although it occupies about one-half of the Florida peninsula, this subspecies has an actual total range of less than one-tenth of that area. This limited range is rapidly being converted into citrus groves, suburbs, and cattle range, and the Florida scrub jay is justifiably listed as "threatened." In addition, it seems unable to tolerate any habitat except thick brush or low trees, and it does not breed until it is two years old.

Like some other members of the crow family, Florida scrub jays are gregarious, and often form affable, noisy groups of a dozen or more birds. They are eager patrons of outdoor feeding stations and become extremely tame and trusting with human encouragement. Their wilderness diet is a widely assorted menu of grasshoppers, wasps, ants, and other insects, and fruit and seeds, particularly sunflower seeds and acorns, which their powerful beaks easily crush. Their nests usually contain from two to five eggs, the average clutch three and a half.

# 13

# Mourning Dove

*(Zenaida macroura)*
"Carolina Turtle Dove"
ABOVE RIGHT, BELOW LEFT: males; ABOVE LEFT, BELOW RIGHT:
females
PLANT:*Steuartia malachodendron*

THOUGH THIS BIRD WAS known to Audubon as the Carolina turtle dove, its modern name is much more appropriate, for it has deep, grieving mating notes and is found throughout the entire United States. The most widespread and familiar dove in North America, it is trimly built and pale gray-brown in color, with a faint green and purple iridescence on the neck—a passenger pigeon in miniature. It is larger than a robin and so swift and erratic in flight that it is ranked close to the bobwhite as an upland game bird in many parts of the South, where it congregates in large flocks during the winter. Northern birders know these dainty, graceful creatures as abundant nesters nearly always seen in congenial pairs and rarely in considerable numbers, until late autumn attracts them to fields where corn or other grain has recently been harvested.

The vast breeding range of the mourning dove runs westward from Nova Scotia to southern New Brunswick and Quebec, through the southern part of central Canada westward to southern British Columbia and the Pacific; from Florida to southern California and Mexico, through Central America to Panama; and, additionally, to the West Indies. There are usually only two eggs to the nest, but these doves may raise two or more broods in a summer—

from as early as April to well into October in the more southerly parts of their breeding territory. The rearing of four broods is not uncommon. Many of these birds remain in the northern states throughout the winter, particularly where suburban feeding stations supply them with wild birdseed mixtures, but their custom of roosting at night in leafless trees invites heavy winter losses from owls and from extreme cold snaps. The majority of mourning doves migrate to winter quarters, which run from central Pennsylvania and northern Ohio, Indiana, and Illinois, southward through Panama.

Great numbers of doves gather at dawn and dusk around western desert water holes and throughout the day in winter grainfields from coast to coast; the hunting kill is tremendous under such circumstances. Like all other pigeons, the mourning dove feeds almost exclusively on seeds, especially those of undesirable weeds. Examinations have shown that an individual dove devours as many as 7,500 small seeds in a few hours. The flight of these doves is noisier than that of most birds—a brassy, startling clatter, combined with a thin, whistling sound that gives an impression of even higher flying speed than the 40 to 50 miles an hour they can easily maintain even on their long migratory missions.

# 14

# *Meadowlark*

*(Sturnella magna* and *Sturnella neglecta)*
ABOVE, AND BELOW LEFT: males; BELOW CENTER AND RIGHT:
females
PLANT: *Gerardia flava*

NOT A LARK AT ALL, but a New World member of the *Icteridae* family, a much larger North American group that includes blackbirds and orioles, the meadowlark is among the earlier spring arrivals in our northern states and one of the latest migrants to head south in autumn. It is also one of the best-loved of American birds, because of the sturdy, golden-breasted beauty of the male meadowlark on his fence post or sapling observation platform and the delightful melody of his whistling song "as fresh and wild as if the wind were blowing through a flute." Meadowlarks build their domed or partially domed cuplike grassy nests on the ground in meadows, and conceal them so well that they are difficult to find. The eggs and young are vulnerable to wholesale destruction, however, when hayfields are mowed and reapers harvest early crops. A heavy toll is also taken by a variety of prowling predators. Not many years ago they were considered game birds and were shot in vast numbers.

The majority of meadowlarks winter deep in the middle and southern states, where their crowding numbers and their fondness for grain still expose them to considerable losses at the hands of hunters and farmers. Actually, they are among the farmer's most valuable allies in the North because their summer food consists almost exclusively of cutworms, grasshoppers, caterpillars, and other insect life, and noxious weed seeds. A recent estimate of the number of grasshoppers fed to ten meadowlark nestlings in a ten-day period was close to seven thousand. In mild winters, many meadowlarks remain late in their nesting range, especially along coastal dunes and marshes, but snowstorms may then kill a large proportion of them; unseasonable spring or fall blizzards occasionally decimate migrating meadowlarks in a few brief days, by blanketing food supplies.

These field birds walk instead of hop as they hunt for insects in the grass. Their flight style is a series of rapid wingbeats alternating with brief glides. Beyond the Plains States, the western meadowlark (*Sturnella neglecta*), which replaces the eastern subspecies (*Sturnella magna*), offers an even more rich and mellow song. In fact, it is often heard above the dialogue, war cries, groans, and laughter on the sound track of a Hollywood movie filmed outdoors—regardless of the supposed setting.

# 15

# Carolina Parakeet

*(Conuropis carolinensis)*
"Carolina Parrot"
FROM TOP: female; male; female; two males; young; female
PLANT: Cocklebur

T O THOSE WHO HAVE SEEN birds of the parrot family only in zoos, living-room cages, and pet shops, as captives from far-off Africa, Australia, and Latin America, it may seem incredible that beautiful green parakeets with fiery red and yellow pates once were abundant native birds in colonial America as far north as New York, Pennsylvania, and Ohio and as far west as Wisconsin, Colorado, and Texas. The Carolina parakeet shown in Audubon's plate was the eastern race of these dove-sized birds. Even during the artist's lifetime, its range shrank rapidly southeastward under ceaseless human persecution. Today, the species is extinct, for none have been reliably reported even in Florida—their last known stand—since 1920, or possibly even earlier.

Like the far more numerous passenger pigeon of a century ago, the Carolina parakeet had very little chance for survival on a continent which the white man had so quickly altered from a wilderness into our present endless panorama of farms, towns, and orchards. As long ago as 1881, a Florida naturalist wrote, "Their enemies are legion. Bird-catchers trap them by hundreds for the northern market. Sportsmen shoot them for food. Planters kill them

because they eat their fruit. Tourists slaughter them simply because they present a favorable mark." Besides all these lethal handicaps, the gorgeous plumage of the Carolina parakeet caught the eyes of milliners throughout the world of fashion; and its own appetite for cultivated corn and other cereals incurred the year-round hostility of farmers. These birds were not hard to kill *en masse;* once a few members of a flock had been shot, their comrades' fatal habit of not deserting the stricken flock members allowed gunners to wipe out their entire number.

The Carolina parakeet traveled about in small, dense groups and apparently even nested in colonies of fifty to a hundred pairs in the hollow trunks of trees. Audubon's picture accurately displays these birds eating the seeds of cockleburs. Upon human settlement, however, the parakeets rapidly transferred their preference from such weeds to cultivated crops and trees, on which our pioneer ancestors depended for their own existence. The last of these magnificent native North American birds was seen in 1920 in an almost inaccessible southern swamp in the Florida Everglades.

# 16

# Whip-poor-will

*(Caprimulgus vociferus)*
ABOVE: male; BELOW: females
PLANT: Black Oak. *Quercus tinctoria*

A BIRD OF THE DEEP DUSK and the deep forest, the whip-poor-will is named for its loud, three-syllable call, which can be recognized instantly even by someone who has never heard it before. Audubon much preferred the sound to the nightingale's song. Probably a thousand people have heard the whip-poor-will for every one who has ever seen it. It is a member of the same family of greatmouths, or night-jars, as the more familiar common nighthawk, but the whip-poor-will seldom rises more than a few yards above the woodland floor on its flights, whereas the nighthawk mounts far into the sunset sky to beat its erratic, careening way above our city parks, skyscrapers, and farms. So furtive is the whip-poor-will that, until 1831, its call was considered the voice of the nighthawk.

In summer it has an immense nesting range, from southern Canada to the southern United States and in the mountains as far south as Mexico. The birds spend the winter months in an area ranging from the Gulf States to Honduras and seldom arrive in our northern states until late May. From then on until August, during the evening and early dawn hours, the area within half a mile of a whip-poor-will's domain resounds with its distinctive call—a strange melancholy note sometimes repeated as often as thirty times a minute and up to a thousand times without noticeable interruption. This nightjar is one of several species that appear to be stimulated to call by moonlight, although the degree of this influence is still being studied by ornithologists.

This mysterious bird is over ten inches long, with a slim, tapering body, a large head, and a huge, almost beakless mouth that can swallow even very large moths. Its mouth is surrounded by stiff sensory hairs that aid the bird in catching flying insects. For better concealment, the whip-poor-will usually perches lengthwise on a branch or log, where its leaf-colored plumage of brown and dark gray blends so perfectly with its surroundings that it is difficult to detect, even at arm's length in daylight. The eggs and young birds are equally well protected by their coloration. Whip-poor-wills are a most valuable control against mosquitoes, grasshoppers, moths, and many other insects.

# 17

# Brown Pelican

*(Pelecanus occidentalis carolinensis)*
Adult male

ONE OF THE MOST spectacular of Florida's wildlife tourist attractions is the huge brown pelican, with its long, pouch-bottomed beak, thick legs reminiscent of *Alice in Wonderland*'s Dodo, solemn eyes, and six-and-one-half-foot wingspread. Audubon himself termed it "one of the most interesting of our American birds," and some of its customs are quite as fascinating as its droll appearance. Thus, in the courtship season, the male walks in circles round and round his intended mate at a sedate, elephantine gait. When the young have hatched, they feed by thrusting their entire head and neck into the parent bird's vast pouch and throat in a manner awesome to observe. Even more interesting in flight than on the ground, these pelicans are highly proficient formation flyers, moving in close order with uniform wing strokes, usually in single file, just above the water. At times they mount almost out of sight to engage in complex evolutions in the sky. Especially thrilling is the brown pelican's fishing style, as it flies downwind from a height of fifteen or twenty feet, to keel over suddenly in a half roll and plunge into a school of fish with a great splash. Invariably the bird emerges from its dive heading upwind—to assure a quick take-off—after hastily swallowing its catch of one or two fair-sized fish, or as many as a score of fingerlings. The pelican's beak-pouch serves as a landing net, and not as a creel or storage tank.

In 1971 the brown pelican was placed on the Endangered Species List of the United States Department of the Interior. It once bred from North Carolina south to Florida and in the warm waters of the Texas and Louisiana Gulf Coast. In 1938 it was estimated that there were from seventy-five thousand to eighty-five thousand brown pelicans inhabiting the Gulf Coast, from Texas to Florida, and the Florida east coast. By 1963, the disappearance of the brown pelican from Louisiana was complete, and there is today only a remnant population on the Texas coast. In Florida it is experiencing reproductive failure and abandoning certain breeding areas. Throughout its existence, this species has been exposed to hurricanes and diseases; a certain number have succumbed to hunters and to long periods of freezing weather. In addition, this bird, having a diet exclusively of fish, collects and stores certain long-lived pesticides which have accumulated, in sublethal concentrations, in the fish's fat tissues. The result is that the reproductive capabilities of the pelican are severely affected. The organochlorines cause changes in the bird's sex hormones, resulting in thin eggshells and aberrant reproductive behavior patterns. The additional stress of the adverse effects induced by other pollutants may be the catalyst that has pushed the brown pelican to the brink of extirpation.

# 18

# Broad-winged Hawk

*(Buteo platypterus)*
ABOVE: male; BELOW: female
PLANT: Pignut. *Juglans porcina*

ONE OF THE MOST abundant birds of prey throughout the wooded regions of eastern North America is the broad-winged hawk. It is also one of the most beneficial to mankind—yet one of the most mercilessly persecuted by gunners. Its diet is confined mainly to rats, mice, and other destructive rodents and to snakes, frogs, and the larvae of large insects. With a length of thirteen to sixteen inches, a wingspread of a yard, and powerful talons, the broad-winged is well equipped to catch and kill weasels and large rats. Poultry, game, and songbirds are seldom pursued, and still more rarely killed, by any of the *Buteo* genus, of which the broad-winged, red-tailed, red-shouldered, Swainson's, and rough-legged hawks are all members. They are slow-flying, soaring birds that make "lazy circles in the sky" and can ride favorable winds up to altitudes of a mile or more. Their style on the wing is quite different from the adroit, fast, "rowing" flight and lightning dive of the falcon and from the low-level, weaving attack of the goshawk and other short-winged hawks. Unlike the larger *Buteo* hawks and the eagles, the broad-winged prefers the woods to open country for its hunting territory. It usually nests well up in a high tree, close to a stream or pond, in hilly or mountainous terrain. Ordinarily, there are only two or three,

rarely four, eggs to the nest. As Audubon noted in his classic life history of these birds, broad-wingeds are quiet, tame, rather inactive hawks, accustomed to perch by the hour on a shaded branch, waiting for quarry to appear nearby.

The broad-winged hawk is a long-distance migrant, spending the summer as far north as central Alberta and Nova Scotia, and wintering from the Florida Keys and southern Mexico to Peru and Brazil. By mid-September, scores of thousands of broad-wingeds are traveling south, riding high on the thermal updrafts and the wind, circling and drifting aloft on almost motionless wings. Usually they are in high-sailing "kettles" (flocks) and follow the inland mountain ridges, which provide optimum contours of flying conditions and the least resistance. On a single day, more than eleven thousand of these hawks have been counted passing over the famous Hawk Mountain, a high "funneling" promontory in the Kittatinny ridges of southern Pennsylvania. Even from New York's 42nd Street or from Chicago's Michigan Avenue, on a cool, dry autumn day, it is often easy to spot dozens of these travelers within an hour, far above the highest buildings, as they follow their ancestral airways down the hemisphere.

# 19

# Gray Catbird

*(Dumetella carolinensis)*
"Catbird"
ABOVE: male; BELOW: female
PLANT: Blackberry. *Rubus villosus*

AUDUBON'S VIVACIOUS painting of the gray catbird was made in New Orleans in 1821, two years after he had abandoned a shaky business career to devote his life to art and nature, but three years before he made his vital decision—at the age of thirty-nine—to paint *all* the *Birds of America* in actual life-size. That task was not completed until 1838, when Audubon was fifty-three years old. Members of the same family of mimics as thrashers and mockingbirds, catbirds have fanned out by late spring over most of North America, from Florida and Texas into Canada and occasionally west of the Rockies. Gray catbirds make themselves welcome in city parks, farmyards, and suburban gardens by their extraordinary vocal mimicry. Typical repertories swing from the feline mew, which suggested its name, to delightful warbled medleys in "linked sweetness long drawn out." Catbirds also offer wonderful imitations of a wide variety of other birds, ranging from a kingfisher's harsh rattle to the gentler notes of swallows, thrushes, and grosbeaks and the clucking of hens. They reputedly even imitate the croaks of frogs and several mechanical sounds.

A tame, inquisitive busybody, smaller and much slimmer than a robin, the catbird sometimes shares the custom of the mockingbird and the Old World nightingale of singing late into the night, and is one of the few birds that can be heard singing well into autumn. These sleek, trim, metallic-colored birds enjoy cultivated fruits and berries, but their depredations are offset by the great numbers of Japanese beetles and various injurious insects they devour. They are famous for their courage in defending their own nests and those of their neighbors against snakes and other intruders, occasionally at the cost of their own lives. They are quick to respond to the cries of young or injured birds and arrive on the scene instantly, fluttering about and voicing plaintive mews until order has been restored. In our northern states, catbirds often raise two broods each summer. The eggs are an extraordinarily beautiful, deep green-blue color. By mid-October, most catbirds are migrating, by a succession of night flights, to their winter range, which extends from southern Mexico and Panama eastward to the Bahamas. In recent years, increased numbers remain in the North through the coldest winter months, living, as such loiterers must, on leftover rations of berries from viburnums, hawthorns, bayberries, and roses.

# 20

# Gray (Canada) Jay

*(Perisoreus canadensis)*
"Canada Jay"
ABOVE: male; BELOW: female
PLANT: White Oak. *Quercus alba*

THIS "ELEGANT JAY, joyous and lively at all times," as Audubon described it, is probably the most abundant winter bird of the Canadian spruce forest, and ranges from northern Labrador and Newfoundland south to Nova Scotia and New Brunswick, across northern New England, New York, and Ontario, through the northern sections of the midwestern and Plains States and of the Northwest Territories, into north central Alaska. It has experienced a range expansion southward into northern California, central Arizona, and southwestern Colorado. In our western mountains it is abundant throughout the year. It is about the same size as our blue jay, but less noisy. Visitors to Yellowstone and other northwestern regions know it also as the Camp Robber or the Whiskey Jack (from its Indian name *wiskedjak*). Its boldness in flying into tents, canoes, cabins, and even campfires to seize food, soap, plug tobacco, or any other object it can carry off, accounts for its reputation as a genial larcenist of the wilderness. It often steals the bait of fur trappers and, unafraid of man, will take food from his hand or fork on the briefest acquaintance.

The gray jay nests as early as February, when temperatures in the north woods are often thirty degrees below zero, and lays its eggs in March or April. From an austere winter diet of lichens, seeds, and carrion, this friendly, cheerful creature turns, in the warmer seasons, to mice, bird's eggs and nestlings, beetles, frogs, caterpillars, nuts, berries, and small reptiles. Like most other jays and crows it is both ravenous and omnivorous, yet it habitually carries away and stores large amounts of nonperishable surplus food for future lean days. In summer, these birds often travel about in loose flocks of thirty or more, harassing owls or foxes they may find and swooping eagerly down at the first sound of an ax or sight of camp smoke, to feast on the woodsman's beans, fish, or game. In spite of their thievish behavior the jays are often regarded with affection by their victims, for the agility, curiosity, and daring of these birds give a welcome touch of life and sound to the empty, ominous loneliness of the forest.

The gray jay is migratory only in the northern area of its range, which reaches the farthest tree limits of arctic Canada and Alaska, and that migration is generally elevational rather than latitudinal. In winters of severe snowfall and food scarcity, rare large-scale southward movements have been recorded, but these are never far below the Canadian border. The gray jay often glides silently from the upper branches of a high tree to the low limb of another and then hops rapidly upward from branch to branch, in a spiral course, only to repeat its gliding routine when it reaches the top.

# 21

# Pileated Woodpecker

*(Dryocopus pileatus)*
ABOVE: adult female; CENTER: adult male; BELOW: young males
PLANT: Raccoon Grape. *Vitis aestivalis*

ONE OF THE GIANTS of its clan, the "logcock," or pileated woodpecker, is so wary that, even in forests where it is common, it is better known to mankind by its work as a lumberman than by personal appearance. Yet it is very conspicuous, almost as large and black as a crow, white-patched, with a wing span of thirty inches and a scarlet crest that flames like a torch as the bird flies across a sunlit clearing. In heavy timber, an occasional living or dead tree may seem to have been perforated by artillery shells and stripped of its bark by a power plane. That tree has been the victim first of destructive, wood-boring ants or other insects and their larvae, and then of pileated woodpeckers attracted by their tenancy. With their powerful beaks the birds seek out the insects to feed on them, to the benefit of neighboring trees. A logcock's dinner tree may show scores of oval or rectangular excavations over six inches long and two inches wide, driven deep into the heart of the tree, with piles of sawdust heaped around its base.

Since the ivory-billed woodpecker is probably extinct, the pileated woodpecker is the largest remaining North American member of the woodpecker family. It is distributed all across North America, from Florida to southeastern Texas and from Quebec to British Columbia. Its four subspecies decrease slightly in size and vary in shade from slaty to sooty black, going from northern to southern specimens. It is not a migratory bird. This impressive creature prefers vast mature stands of coniferous and mixed woods, especially dense forests where there is a high percentage of dead stumps, and also forest borders. The pileated woodpecker has become more numerous recently in the northeastern states, owing to its ability to acclimate to civilization, and is no longer shot as game. Its call is a resonant, rolling drumbeat that can be heard from an astonishing distance. Like other woodpeckers, it excavates its own nest hole by boring into and then down inside the trunk of a tree to a depth of up to two feet.

# 22

# Trumpeter Swan

*(Olor buccinator)*
Adult

THE TRUMPETER IS the largest, heaviest, and most magnificent of American wildfowl, with a total length of six feet and a wing span of up to eight feet. The swan is so named because it has a deep, resonant French-horn quality to its voice, produced by its very elongated windpipe, which has a high, upward loop as it enters the breastbone. The bird weighs approximately thirty-eight pounds—about three times the weight of a large eagle.

In Audubon's lifetime these beautiful swans were probably fairly common in central and western North America. Both their numbers and their range shrank alarmingly after the turn of the century, but both the United States and Canada have made vigorous efforts to preserve the remaining trumpeters and are to be congratulated for a remarkable propagation of the species. Of the remaining breeding trumpeters, more than one thousand pairs now live in western North America between 40° and 65° N latitude and in a few scattered shallow-water lakes, streams, and ponds in Idaho, Montana, and Wyoming. There are also approximately forty to fifty pairs breeding in northwestern Alberta, probably five hundred or six hundred birds spread throughout the frozen waters of interior British Columbia, and a few hundred more in Alaska. Wherever possible they are under stringent warden protection against hunters, wolves, coyotes, and other predators. However, largely because they winter far to the north, they face the risk of heavy mortality through freeze-ups on the mountain lakes where they still survive. By contrast, the very similar whistling swan remains abundant and widely distrib-

uted and has resisted extinction more successfully.

The trumpeter and whistling swans are not easy to distinguish in the wild, and both also resemble the mute swan. The trumpeter swan is a fresh-water species that Audubon found in great numbers along the lower Mississippi in winter, their bugling cries ringing out of the sky from a great height as they circled down to alight. The whistling swan prefers coastal and tidal waters and winters over a large area in the South. It is further protected by the fact that it nests in the high Arctic, remote from human enemies, and so early in the spring that deep snow still remains on the tundra. Thus even Indians and Eskimos are rarely able to find them. The trumpeter swan never developed the wary customs of the whistlers, and was easily shot. Since it nests where fresh-water bodies are shallow, stable in level, and surrounded by solitude, its eggs and downy young are also exposed to attack by crows, ravens, and other predators. Its nests generally contain three to nine off-white eggs. Swans are mainly herbivorous. They cannot dive, but by tipping their long necks forward they can browse among the stems and roots of water plants two or three feet below the surface.

In earlier days the trumpeters were shot both as game and for their valuable down, feathers, and quills, but they are now fully protected in the United States and Canada. In 1971, after almost forty years on the Endangered Species List, the stock was estimated to be at a safe maintenance level and so was removed. There is cause for optimism in this example of population recovery.

# 23

# *Wood Duck*

*(Aix sponsa)*
LEFT: males; RIGHT: females
PLANT: Buttonwood Tree. *Platanus occidentalis*

NO OTHER WATERFOWL in the world rivals the drake wood duck in beauty. Even the dainty mandarin duck of Asia cannot match its brilliant, richly patterned plumage, its delicately graceful form, and the silent, meteor-like magic of its flight. The wood duck is exclusively a North American bird; its summer and winter ranges are largely confined to the United States. The entire North American wood duck population winters within the borders of the United States, with an occasional vagrant recorded in Mexico. At one time close to extermination, these exquisite birds were saved only by rigorous hunting restrictions. They have recently increased in numbers and enjoy a stable population. Audubon's painting of the wood duck was made in West Feliciana Parish, Louisiana, in 1825, when he had reached the superb maturity of his style. It ranks among the more decorative and aesthetically pleasing of the 435 Elephant Folio prints.

The wood duck's name comes from its habit—unusual among waterfowl—of living among fresh-water woodland ponds and streams and nesting in hollow trees or branches, between twenty and fifty feet above ground. There are from thirteen to sixteen eggs to the nest in a normal complete clutch. Within a day after they hatch, the downy young clamber on needle-sharp claws to the entrance of the nest, prompted by a series of low soft calls from the mother, stationed below the nest. They leap out, one by one, and parachute to earth on tiny stub wings. One such mass drop took place from a nest hole twenty-two feet above a concrete sidewalk. The ducklings bounced several inches, yet none was injured by the fall. Once the mother wood duck has assembled her airborne brood, she leads them to the water nearest the hatching place for the remainder of their infancy.

Unlike most waterfowl, wood ducks often feed on dry land, hunting for acorns, berries, nuts, and insects. Their aquatic fare includes wild rice, duckweed, and tadpoles. These beautiful birds are preyed upon by a variety of enemies. Black snakes, opossums, and raccoons take a heavy toll of the eggs. Snapping turtles, pike, and other large fish, as well as snakes and predatory birds and mammals, can reduce the brood size substantially during the fledging period. In the South, garfish and alligators often attack even the adult wood ducks.

# 24

# Belted Kingfisher

*(Megaceryle alcyon)*
ABOVE, AND BELOW LEFT: males; BELOW RIGHT: female

A LEGEND OF ANCIENT Greece tells of a great storm in which Ceyx, king of Thessaly and son of the Morning Star, was drowned in a shipwreck. So deep was the grief of his queen, Halcyone, that the gods on Olympus took pity on the royal pair, and turned them both into *halcyons*, or kingfishers. The alleged weather control exerted by these birds was so powerful that they could calm the wild Aegean Sea during "halcyon days" each year, while their seaborne, floating nest held their brood! And today, *halcyon* is the root word from which are derived both the scientific name of our belted kingfisher and also the general Greek name for the worldwide family of more than eighty varieties of kingfishers—the *Alcedinidae*. They vary in size from the four-inch pygmy kingfisher to the giant kookaburra (laughing jackass) of Australia, and most of them live on islands of the South Pacific.

The belted kingfisher ranges in summer throughout most of North America, from central Alaska, across Canada, and south to Mexico. Most of them migrate in cold weather, some as far as Panama and the West Indies, but a few remain as far north as the limit of open-water sites—that is, river mouths, lake shores, and fast-running streams—even in New England. Contrary to the lovely Greek legend, kingfishers actually nest in deep burrows, four to five feet long, which they tunnel horizontally into streamside sand or gravel banks. They deposit their eggs in an unlined chamber at the end of the tunnel, safe from most predators. Their broods are large and usually contain from five to eight young. They feed mainly on small fish of minnow size, catching them by a vertical dive into the water after hovering briefly in flight or plunging from an overhanging tree limb. In this pursuit, the kingfisher's spearlike, powerful beak is useful. When fish are scarce, mice, frogs, crayfish, insects, and even fruit are also taken. While belted kingfishers are thoroughly unwelcome near fish hatcheries, they perform a useful task in the wild by enabling the reduced numbers of surviving fish to grow faster on the available food supply.

With its big tousled head, bushy crest, large dagger-like bill, and slaty-blue back, the pigeon-sized belted kingfisher is not easily mistaken for any other bird. Its dry, prolonged, penetrating rattle is unique. Both sexes wear a blue collar but the female also has a chestnut belly band across her white breast, like that of the bird swallowing a fish in Audubon's plate. The ringed kingfisher of southern Texas and the little green kingfisher of the far Southwest are the only other *halcyons* found in the United States.

# 25

# Yellow-breasted Chat

*(Icteria virens)*
Female in nest; others males
PLANT: Sweet Briar. *Rosa rubiginosa*

LARGEST MEMBER OF the extensive New World family of wood warblers, the chat is one of the most talented clowns of the feathered kingdom, both with its voice and with its droll antics in the air. Rising from his perch in some thick bush or briar patch, the male flops about in an awkward fashion, with his legs dangling, and performs parachute-like descents on uptilted wings while jerking his tail. This "performing," as Audubon quaintly noted long ago, involves "the strangest and most whimsical gesticulations." Equally amazing are the loud sounds uttered by this beautiful creature, ranging from caws, gobbles, mews, barks, and whinnies to squawks, whistles, and an assortment of rather musical phrases. The yellow-breasted chat is so shy and conceals itself so well in dense cover that few people ever catch sight of it, even though it is brilliantly colored and is often found nesting close to farms and suburban homes. This bird's ventriloquial skill also makes it difficult to locate by ear and gives the listener the impression that a dozen birds of different kinds are competing, far and near all around him, for some woodland meistersinger's prize. The chat occa-sionally sings at night, as do the mockingbird, American woodcock, whip-poor-will, snipe, and owl; most of these birds confine their nocturnes to early evening or to bright, moonlit nights.

The chat's summer domain extends across the United States from coast to coast, north into southern Canada and south into Mexico. It prefers to live in tangled, impenetrable thickets and hedgerows along streams, rather than in open country or in high trees. The brood usually numbers four or five nestlings. While mainly insectivorous, the chat is also fond of ripe berries and so must follow the sun with the seasons to keep supplied with food. It seldom reaches our northern states until May and begins moving south in early autumn, to spend the winter in Mexico and Central America as far south as Panama. As John Burroughs wrote in *Wake-Robin*, the yellow-breasted chat "is truly an original. The cat-bird is mild and feminine compared with this rollick-ing polyglot. His voice is very loud and strong and quite uncanny." Fortunate indeed is the rural family that can share mellow midsummer days and evenings in the close company of this entertaining little bird.

# 26

# Mallard

*(Anas platyrhynchos)*
FROM LEFT: first and third, females; second and fourth, males

ONE OF THE MOST widely distributed, most abundant, and most important to mankind of all the ducks, the "greenhead" in its wild state is found in most parts of North America, Iceland, Greenland, Europe, and Asia. It is large and easily domesticated, and was a progenitor of many of the varieties of domestic duck. It often hybridizes with the black duck and less frequently with other wild species such as the pintail, gadwall, Mexican duck, and mottled duck. No waterfowl except the canvasback outranks the mallard in the esteem of American sportsmen and cosmopolitan gourmets. In China, for thousands of years, its meat and eggs have been major items in the food supply.

American mallards nest mainly from the Canadian prairie provinces north into Alaska. They winter throughout a vast area, from the Aleutians and open-water subarctic regions all across the United States south to the Gulf Coast and central Mexico, with an abundant stronghold in the lower Mississippi Valley. Audubon described the cackling of mallards "which would almost deafen you" in the Kentucky sloughs and the mating display of the drake with "his silken head and honeyed jabbering." Mallards are vociferous quackers at all seasons, but particularly in early spring, when they are among the first waterfowl arrivals, close behind the retreating barrier of ice.

Although largely herbivorous, mallards prefer the larvae of mosquitoes to any other summer fare. Their flying speed has been clocked at 45 to 60 miles an hour, which is exceeded by only a few other ducks. The average nest contains eight or ten eggs, but the depredations of crows and raccoons on the eggs and of snapping turtles and large fish on the ducklings usually do not leave a great surplus in the breeding stock for the benefit of sportsmen. A dry summer in Canada is an even greater danger to this species. It forces the hens to take their broods on long death marches seeking open water. The hot sun in combination with predatory animals destroys a great many of them. The drakes take no part in the labor of incubating the eggs and raising the ducklings, but gather in small stag flocks early in the summer.

# 27

# Cardinal

*(Cardinalis cardinalis)*
"Cardinal Grosbeak"
ABOVE: male; BELOW: female
PLANT: Wild Almond

WELL NAMED FOR ITS mitre-like crest and for the deep, rich red plumage of the male bird, the cardinal is among the largest and most conspicuous members of the vast finch family. More specifically, it is one of the grosbeaks, whose short, thick, powerful cone-shaped bills and large jaw muscles enable them to crush the shells of seeds and nuts too hard for most birds to crack. This redbird is among the most popular because of its glowing beauty and the variety of its vocal repertory, which ranges from clear whooping whistles to flinty metallic chirps of alarm and a rich chain of brief warbles. It is not surprising that the cardinal is the state bird of a larger number of states than any other species—the list includes Illinois, Indiana, Kentucky, North Carolina, Ohio, Virginia, and West Virginia—or that a National League baseball team has chosen this bird for its emblem.

Cardinals are not migratory. Many of them spend their lives year-round within a few miles of where they were hatched, but they do wander about in search of suitable feeding territory. They have undergone a very considerable range extension northward in the past few decades, and are now common to abundant in most of northern New England and southern Canada, where they were almost unknown before 1950. A pattern of mild winters and the dramatic increase of feeding stations, well supplied throughout the winter, are certainly major factors in this expansion.

Cardinals prefer low underbrush, swamps, and the edge of woodlands, and they avoid the deep forest as well as the treeless plains. Although they come readily to feeders where sunflower seeds are provided, they do seem to dislike exposing themselves to long flights in the open in broad daylight—perhaps aware that their flashing color and slow flying speed make them easy prey for hungry hawks. Possibly for the same reason, they feed earlier in the morning and later in the evening than most songsters. Cardinals are early nesters even in the northern states, and many of them undertake their first nest before mid-April. They usually raise two broods each year, with three or four eggs to the nest. Audubon's painting of the cardinal was made in Louisiana in 1821, midway in his career as a bird artist.

# 28

# Baltimore (Northern) Oriole

*(Icterus galbula)*
LEFT: female; RIGHT: males
PLANT: Yellow Poplar. *Liriodendron tulipifera*

TOUCHES OF FLAME shuttling about in our northern town and orchard trees in early May signal the return from the tropics of one of North America's most beautiful songbirds. With his fiery orange breast, black head, and orange-and-black tail touched with white, the male Baltimore oriole is rarely surpassed for sheer splendor. The British colonist Lord Baltimore, whose family colors were black and orange, is its namesake. Another of the bird's attractive features is its bright, warbling song. Astonishingly loud and interspersed with chattering notes, this warbling advertises the ownership of a specific territory. Both male and female orioles sing, which helps viewers on the ground who seek out the regal male and his less brilliant mate in the topmost branches of trees.

As distinctive as the color and melody of this oriole are, its deep, purselike gray nest has also won it merited claim. It is, in fact, a hanging pouch with its four to six eggs laid at the expanded bottom of the six-inch sac. In the hot South the nest is artfully woven so that it is porous and fibrous, for air-conditioning. In the North the fibers are more tightly knotted for warmth and insulation. The nest is placed very high in a tree and usually swings from an outer branch of an elm or maple where it is easily seen yet safe from predators. This species is notable for returning each spring to the same neighborhood, and even to the same nesting tree, after a winter spent as far away as Peru or Colombia. Ordinarily, a new and complex nest is constructed each year, even though each is so durably built that winter may reveal three or four nests from previous seasons in the same leafless tree.

Orioles belong to the large family of icterids, which also includes grackles, bobolinks, meadowlarks, cowbirds, and other blackbirds. The Baltimore race of the northern oriole occupies a vast breeding range, from northern Georgia to Nova Scotia, and west to Texas and Alberta. It is replaced by its counterpart, the Bullock's race, in the Far West. While both are mainly insect-eating birds, they will occasionally eat fruit and berries. It is a real treat to observe an oriole delicately pierce the skin of a cherry with his beak and gracefully sip its juice.

In the evolution of bird migration, it is probable that some varieties of brilliantly colored birds originally native to the tropics—among them, the orioles—extended their spring flights farther and farther north. Correspondingly, scores of arctic birds, driven south during the Ice Age, merely returned to the North as the glaciers withdrew and, even today, never migrate as far south as the tropics.

# Greater Flamingo

*(Phoenicopterus ruber)*
"American Flamingo"
Old male

T HIS LARGEST OF the brilliantly colored birds of the New World, formerly called the American flamingo, is partially related to herons and partially to swans. It is about four feet in length and has a wingspan of more than five feet. The greater flamingo is now in danger of extermination by man, for the adults are still being killed for their gorgeous feathers and the young are hunted for food. During World War II, whole colonies of flamingos were driven from their ancient haunts in the Bahamas by low-flying training planes. Many other colonies were abandoned when oil-drilling crews invaded their vicinity. Greater flamingos occupy a vast, scattered range through southeastern Mexico, the West Indies, the Bahamas, the islands off Venezuela, and the mainland coast from Yucatán to Brazil. Audubon saw a few flocks of the strange, web-footed birds in the Florida Keys in 1832. Now, only an occasional wanderer reaches south Florida, Hispaniola, and our southernmost islands in the Gulf of Mexico.

The feeding procedure of flamingos is highly specialized, the sickle-shaped beak being used to scoop small shellfish from the floor of shallow lagoons. To secure its prey, the bird plunges its head underwater upside down, the upper bill serving as a dredge and the tongue as a sieve. Flamingos live in dense flocks the year around. The nests, in congested colonies, are flat-topped cones, built up to a height of a foot or more, from pellets of marl bitten out of the surrounding soil. More than two thousand such nests, each holding only one egg, have been counted in a single community covering barely half an acre. The chicks move about a few hours after hatching, and gather in amiable, nursery-like groups, or crèches, to be fed by their elders.

An observer on the Cape Sable tip of Florida in 1890 described a flock of more than one thousand flamingos as a "bank of rosy, fire-like color" stretching evenly along the shore for three-quarters of a mile. As the birds prepared to fly away, the line contracted toward the center. "Soon they were in full flight, a cloud of flame-colored pink, like the hues of a brilliant sunset." On the wing, flamingos move low over the water, in single file or in V-formations, seeming to crawl laboriously through the air as their long necks undulate in rhythm with their wing strokes. Superstitious Spanish explorers considered the birds flying crosses and protected their eggs. Flamingos of four other species are found in Africa, southern Europe, Asia, and in South America, where the rare James flamingo nests on lakes fed by hot springs high in the Andes.

# *Painted Bunting*

*(Passerina ciris)*
"Painted Finch"
FROM BOTTOM, CLOCKWISE: two old males; male, first year;
female; male, second year
PLANT: *Prunus chicasa*

FEW WILD BIRDS OF North America wear such a variety of gorgeous colors as the mature male nonpareil, as this bunting is also called. Audubon's plate purposely displays two male plumages—the dull second-year coat and the rich blue-violet, red, scarlet, and yellow-green of a bird two or more years old. So pugnacious are these finches in the mating season that two fighting males can sometimes be caught on the ground by hand, without stopping their savage head-pecking. This belligerence was also the secret of the trapping method formerly used to catch thousands of painted buntings every year so that they could be sold as pets, since they are as attractive for their song as for their coat of many colors. These beautiful little birds were captured by setting a cage occupied by a stuffed male bunting in an open space, where, by Audubon's quaint account: "A male painted finch passes over it, perceives it, and dives towards it with all the anger which its little breast can contain. It alights on the edge of the trap and, throwing its body against the stuffed bird, brings down the trap and is made prisoner." Such a captive, worth only a few cents in the New Orleans market, was sold in Great Britain and on the Continent for as much as fifteen dollars!

Painted buntings prefer thickets, hedgerows, and the shrubbery of city gardens, where there is an abundance of dense cover. Their food is weed and grain seed, cotton worms and weevils, and other small insects. The male spends most of his summer daylight hours singing his pleasant song from a treetop or power line. His mate, like the female indigo bunting, leads a quiet existence in the underbrush. Even in summer, nonpareils seldom come further north than southeastern North Carolina and are common only in the deep southern states, from northern Florida to New Mexico. In autumn, they retire to southern Florida and Louisiana, the Bahamas, Cuba, and Panama. The nesting season is from mid-May to late July, two broods often being raised, in well-hidden nests, usually less than six feet above the ground. Even for people who have seen painted buntings close at hand for many years, there is always the thrill of fresh discovery at the sight of one of these brilliant finches glowing in the light of a cloudless day.

# Illustrated Catalogue

## of

# The Birds of America

1

2

3

1 Californian Turkey Vulture
 (*Gymnogyps californianus*)
 "Californian Vulture"

2 Red-headed Turkey Vulture
 (*Cathartes aura*)
 "Turkey Buzzard"

3 Black Vulture or Carrion Crow
 (*Coragyps atratus*)

4 Caracara Eagle
 (*Caracara cheriway*)
 "Caracara"

5 Harris' Buzzard
 (*Parabuteo unicinctus*)
 "Louisiana Hawk"

6 Common Buzzard
 (*Buteo swainsoni*)

7 Red-tailed Buzzard
 (*Buteo jamaicensis*)
 "Red-tailed Hawk"

8 Harlan's Buzzard
 (*Buteo harlani*)
 "Black Warrior"

9 Red-shouldered Buzzard
 (*Buteo lineatus*)
 "Red-shouldered Hawk"

10 Broad-winged Buzzard [Hawk]
 See Havell colorplate 18

The 1871 edition of *The Birds of America* contains five hundred plates lithographed by J. T. Bowen of Philadelphia, after the originals by Audubon. All five hundred plates, numbered as in the 1871 edition, are catalogued in the following pages, and four hundred and seventy are illustrated. The thirty birds not illustrated are those for which we have already presented Havell colorplates in the "Thirty Great Audubon Birds" section of this volume. A cross-reference at the appropriate Bowen number directs the reader to the corresponding Havell plate.

The entry for each plate contains the following information: the name of the bird as given on the plate; its Latin designation; its name in Audubon's *Ornithological Biography*, if that differs by more than spelling from the name on the plate; and identification of sexes, plant life, other animals, and settings, when these are given on the Bowen plate.

4

5

6

7

8

9

11                                                    12

15                            16                            17

20

21

13

14

18

11 Rough-legged Buzzard
   (*Buteo lagopus*)
   "Rough-legged Falcon"

12 Golden Eagle
   (*Aquila chrysaetos*)

13 Washington Sea Eagle
   (*Haliaeetus leucocephalus*)
   "Bird of Washington"

14 White-headed Sea Eagle or Bald Eagle
   (*Haliaeetus leucocephalus*)
   "White-headed Eagle"

15 Common Osprey—Fish Hawk
   (*Pandion haliaetus*)
   "Fish Hawk"

16 Black-shouldered Elanus
   (*Elanus leucurus*)
   "Black-shouldered Hawk"

17 Mississippi Kite
   (*Ictinia misisippiensis*)

18 Swallow-tailed Hawk
   (*Elanoides forficatus*)

19 Iceland or Gyre Falcon
   See Havell colorplate 9

20 Peregrine Falcon
   (*Falco peregrinus*)
   "Great-footed Hawk"

21 Pigeon Falcon
   (*Falco columbarius*)
   ABOVE: "Pigeon Hawk";
   BELOW: "Le Petit Caporal"

22 Sparrow Falcon
   (*Falco sparverius*)
   "American Sparrow Hawk"

22

23

23 Gos Hawk
   (*Accipiter gentilis*)

24

25

26

30

31

35

36

27

28

29

32

33

34

24 Cooper's Hawk
   (*Accipiter cooperii*)
   "Stanley Hawk"

25 Sharp-shinned Hawk
   (*Accipiter striatus*)

26 Common Harrier
   (*Circus cyaneus*)
   "Marsh Hawk"

27 Hawk Owl
   (*Surnia ulula*)

28 Snowy Owl
   (*Nyctea scandiaca*)

29 Passerine Day Owl
   (*Athene noctua*)
   "Little Night Owl"

30 Columbian Day Owl
   (*Glaucidium gnoma*)
   "Little Columbian Owl"

31 Burrowing Day Owl
   (*Speotyto cunicularia*)

32 Tengmalm's Night Owl
   (*Aegolius funereus*)

33 Little or Acadian Owl
   (*Aegolius acadicus*)
   Common Mouse

34 Barn Owl
   (*Tyto alba*)

35 Great Cinereous Owl
   (*Strix nebulosa*)

36 Barred Owl
   (*Strix varia*)

38

37

44

48

37  Long-eared Owl
    *(Asio otus)*

38  Short-eared Owl
    *(Asio flammeus)*

39  Great Horned Owl
    *(Bubo virginianus)*

40  Little Screech Owl
    See Havell colorplate 5

41  Chuck-will's Widow
    *(Caprimulgus carolinensis)*
    Harlequin Snake

42  Whip-poor-will
    See Havell colorplate 16

43  Night Hawk
    *(Chordeiles minor)*
    PLANT: White Oak. *Quercus alba*

44  American Swift
    *(Chaetura pelagica)*
    "Chimney Swallow or American Swift"
    Nests

45  Purple Martin
    *(Progne subis)*
    PLANT: Calabash

46  White-bellied Swallow
    *(Iridoprocne bicolor)*

47  Cliff Swallow
    *(Petrochelidon pyrrhonota)*
    "Republican or Cliff Swallow"
    Nests

48  Barn or Chimney Swallow
    *(Hirundo rustica)*
    "Barn Swallow"

49  Violet-green Swallow
    *(Tachycineta thalassina)*

50  Bank Swallow
    *(Riparia riparia)*

51  Rough-winged Swallow
    *(Stelgidopteryx ruficollis)*

39

41

43

45

46

47

49

50

51

52

53

54

55

52 Fork-tailed Flycatcher
(*Muscivora tyrannus*)
PLANT: *Gordonia lasianthus*

53 Swallow-tailed Flycatcher
(*Muscivora forficata*)

54 Arkansas Flycatcher
(*Tyrannus verticalis*)

55 Pipiry Flycatcher
(*Tyrranus dominicensis*)
PLANT: *Agati grandiflora*

56 Tyrant Flycatcher or King Bird
(*Tyrranus tyrannus*)
PLANT: Cottonwood. *Populus candicans*

57 Great Crested Flycatcher
(*Myiarchus crinitus*)

58 Cooper's Flycatcher
(*Nuttallornis borealis*)
"Olive-sided Flycatcher"
ABOVE: female; BELOW: male
PLANT: Balsam or Silver Fir.
*Pinus balsamea*

59 Say's Flycatcher
(*Sayornis saya*)
LEFT: male; RIGHT: female

60 Rocky Mountain Flycatcher
(*Sayornis nigricans*)
Male
PLANT: Swamp Oak. *Quercus aquatica*

56

57

58

59

60

61

62

65

66

67

70

63

64

68

69

71

72

61 Short-legged Pewit Flycatcher
(*Contopus sordidulus*)
Male
PLANT: Hobble Bush. *Vibernum lantanerdes*

62 Small Green-crested Flycatcher
(*Empidonax virescens*)
ABOVE: male; BELOW: female
PLANT: Sassafras. *Laurus sassafras*

63 Pewee Flycatcher
(*Sayornis phoebe*)
ABOVE: male; BELOW: female
PLANT: Cotton Plant. *Gossypium herbaceum*

64 Wood Pewee Flycatcher
(*Contopus virens*)
"Wood Pewee"
Male
PLANT: Swamp Honeysuckle. *Azalea viscosa*

65 Traill's Flycatcher
(*Empidonax traillii*)
Male
PLANT: Sweet Gum. *Liquidambar styracifolia*

66 Least Pewee Flycatcher
(*Empidonax minimus*)
"Little Tyrant Flycatcher"
Male
PLANT: White Oak. *Quercus primus*

67 Small-headed Flycatcher
(*Muscicapa minuta*)
Male
PLANT: Virginian Spider-wort.
*Tradescantia virginica*

68 American Redstart
(*Setophaga ruticilla*)
ABOVE: female; BELOW: male
PLANT: Virginian Hornbeam or Iron-wood Tree

69 Townsend's Ptilogonys
(*Myadestes townsendi*)
Female

70 Blue-gray Flycatcher
(*Polioptila caerulea*)
ABOVE: male; BELOW: female
PLANT: Black Walnut. *Juglans nigra*

71 Hooded Flycatching Warbler
(*Wilsonia citrina*)
"Hooded Warbler"
ABOVE: female; BELOW: male
PLANT: *Erithryna herbacea*

72 Canada Flycatcher
(*Wilsonia canadensis*)
ABOVE: male; BELOW: female
PLANT: Great Laurel. *Rhododendron maximum*

73

74

75

79

80

81

73 Bonaparte's Flycatching Warbler
   (*Wilsonia canadensis*)
   "Bonaparte's Fly-catcher"
   Male
   PLANT: Great Magnolia. *Magnolia grandiflora*

74 Kentucky Flycatching Warbler
   (*Oporornis formosus*)
   "Kentucky Warbler"
   ABOVE: female; BELOW: male
   PLANT: *Magnolia auriculata*

75 Wilson's Flycatching Warbler
   (*Wilsonia pusilla*)
   "Green Black-capped Flycatcher"
   ABOVE: female; BELOW: male
   PLANT: Snake's Head. *Chelone glabra*

76 Yellow-crowned Wood Warbler
   (*Dendroica coronata*)
   "Yellow-rump Warbler"
   ABOVE: male; BELOW: young
   PLANT: *Iris versicolor*

77 Audubon's Wood Warbler
   (*Dendroica auduboni*)
   ABOVE: male; BELOW: female
   PLANT: Strawberry Tree. *Euonymus americanus*

78 Black-poll Wood Warbler
   (*Dendroica striata*)
   "Black-poll Warbler"
   ABOVE: female; CENTER AND BELOW: males
   PLANT: Black Gum Tree. *Nyssa aquatica*

76

77

78

82

83

84

79 Yellow-throated Wood Warbler
   *(Dendroica dominica)*
   "Yellow-throated Warbler"
   Male
   PLANT: Chinquapin. *Castanea pumila*

80 Bay-breasted Wood Warbler
   *(Dendroica castanea)*
   "Bay-breasted Warbler"
   ABOVE: male; BELOW: female
   PLANT: Highland Cotton Plant. *Gossipium herbaceum*

81 Chestnut-sided Wood Warbler
   *(Dendroica pensylvanica)*
   "Chestnut-sided Warbler"
   ABOVE: female; BELOW: male
   PLANT: Moth Mullein. *Verbascum blattaria*

82 Pine-creeping Wood Warbler
   *(Dendroica pinus)*
   "Pine Creeping Warbler"
   ABOVE: male; BELOW: female
   PLANT: Yellow Pine. *Pinus variabilis*

83 Hemlock Warbler
   *(Dendroica fusca)*
   ABOVE: female; BELOW: male
   PLANT: Dwarf Maple. *Acer spicatum*

84 Black-throated Green Wood Warbler
   *(Dendroica virens)*
   "Black-throated Green Warbler"
   ABOVE: male; BELOW: female
   PLANT: *Caprifolium sempervirens*

85

86

87

91

92

85 Cape May Wood Warbler
(*Dendroica tigrina*)
"Cape May Warbler"
ABOVE: male; BELOW: female

86 Cerulean Wood Warbler
(*Dendroica cerulea*)
"Azure Warbler" or "Blue-green Warbler"
ABOVE: old male; BELOW: young male
PLANTS: Bear-berry and Spanish Mulberry

87 Blackburnian Wood Warbler
(*Dendroica fusca*)
"Blackburnian Warbler"
ABOVE: female; BELOW: male
PLANT: *Phlox maculata*

88 Yellow-poll Wood Warbler
(*Dendroica petechia*)
"Yellow-poll Warbler"
Males

89 Rathbone's Wood Warbler
(*Dendroica petechia*)
"Rathbone Warbler"
ABOVE: male; BELOW: female
PLANT: Ramping Trumpet Flower

90 Yellow Redpoll Wood Warbler
(*Dendroica palmarum*)
"Yellow Redpoll Warbler"
ABOVE AND CENTER: males; BELOW: young
PLANT: Wild Orange Tree

88

89

90

93

94

95

91  Blue Yellow-backed Wood Warbler
    *(Parula americana)*
    "Blue Yellow-back Warbler"
    ABOVE: male; BELOW: female
    PLANT: Louisiana Flag

92  Townsend's Wood Warbler
    *(Dendroica townsendi)*
    "Townsend's Warbler"
    Male
    PLANT: Carolina Allspice

93  Hermit Wood Warbler
    *(Dendroica occidentalis)*
    "Hermit Warbler"
    ABOVE: female; BELOW: male
    PLANT: Strawberry Tree

94  Black-throated Gray Wood Warbler
    *(Dendroica nigrescens)*
    "Black-throated Grey Warbler"
    Males

95  Black-throated Blue Wood Warbler
    *(Dendroica caerulescens)*
    "Pine Swamp Warbler"
    ABOVE: male; BELOW: female
    PLANT: Canadian Columbine

96 Black-and-yellow Wood Warbler
(*Dendroica magnolia*)
"Black and Yellow Warbler"
ABOVE: young; CENTER: male; BELOW: female
PLANT: Flowering Raspberry. *Rubus odoratus*

97 Prairie Wood Warbler
(*Dendroica discolor*)
"Prairie Warbler"
ABOVE: female; BELOW: male
PLANT: Buffalo Grass

98 Blue Mountain Warbler
(*Dendroica montana*)
Male

99 Connecticut Warbler
(*Oporornis agilis*)
ABOVE: female; BELOW: male
PLANT: *Gentiana saponaria*

100 Macgillivray's Ground Warbler
(*Oporornis tolmiei*)
"Macgillivray's Warbler"
ABOVE: male; BELOW: female

101 Mourning Ground Warbler
(*Trichas philadelphia*)
Male
PLANT: Pheasant's Eye. *Flos adonis*

96

97

101

102

104

105

106

98 99 100

103

107

102 Maryland Ground Warbler
*(Geothlypis trichas)*
"Maryland Yellow-throat"
ABOVE: young male; CENTER: adult male; BELOW: female
PLANT: Wild Olive

103 Delafield's Ground Warbler
*(Trichas delafieldii)*
Male

104 Swainson's Swamp Warbler
*(Limnothlypis swainsonii)*
"Swainson's Warbler"
Male
PLANT: Orange-colored Azalea. *Azalea calendulacea*

105 Worm-eating Swamp Warbler
*(Helmitheros vermivorus)*
"Worm-eating Warbler"
ABOVE: male; BELOW: female
PLANT: American Poke-weed. *Phytolacca decandra*

106 Prothonotary Swamp Warbler
*(Protonotaria citrea)*
"Prothonotary Warbler"
ABOVE: male; BELOW: female
PLANT: Cane Vine

107 Golden-winged Swamp Warbler
*(Vermivora chrysoptera)*
"Golden-winged Warbler"
ABOVE: female; BELOW: male

108

109

110

114

115

116

108 Bachman's Swamp Warbler
(*Vermivora bachmanii*)
"Bachman's Warbler"
ABOVE: male; BELOW: female
PLANT: *Gordonia pubescens*

109 Carbonated Swamp Warbler
(*Dendroica carbonata*)
Males
PLANT: May-bush or Service. *Pyrus botryapium*

110 Tennessee Swamp Warbler
(*Vermivora peregrina*)
"Tennessee Warbler"
Male
PLANT: *Ilex laxifolia*

111 Blue-winged Yellow Swamp Warbler
(*Vermivora pinus*)
"Blue-winged Yellow Warbler"
ABOVE: male; BELOW: female
PLANT: Cotton Rose. *Hibiscus grandiflorus*

112 Orange-crowned Swamp Warbler
(*Vermivora celata*)
"Orange-crowned Warbler"
ABOVE: female; BELOW: male
PLANT: Huckleberry. *Vaccinium frondosum*

113 Nashville Swamp Warbler
(*Vermivora ruficapilla*)
"Nashville Warbler"
ABOVE: female; BELOW: male
PLANT: Swamp Spice

111

112

113

117

118

119

114 Black-and-white Creeping Warbler
*(Mniotilta varia)*
"Black-and-white Creeper"
Male
PLANT: Black Larch. *Pinus pendula*

115 Brown Tree-creeper
*(Certhia familiaris)*
"Brown Creeper"
ABOVE: female; BELOW: male

116 Rock Wren
*(Salpinctes obsoletus)*
Adult female
PLANT: *Smilacina borealis*

117 Great Carolina Wren
*(Thryothorus ludovicianus)*
ABOVE: male; BELOW: female
PLANT: Dwarf Buckeye. *Asculus pavia*

118 Bewick's Wren
*(Thryomanes bewickii)*
Male
PLANT: Iron-wood Tree

119 Wood Wren
*(Troglodytes aedon)*
Male
PLANT: Arbutus. *Uva ursi*

120

121

122

124

125

126

128

129

130

123

127

120 House Wren
*(Troglodytes aedon)*
ABOVE: male; BELOW, LEFT: female; BELOW, RIGHT; young
In an old Hat

121 Winter Wren
*(Troglodytes troglodytes)*
ABOVE: young; BELOW, LEFT: female; BELOW, RIGHT: male

122 Parkman's Wren
*(Troglodytes parkmanii)*
Male
PLANT: *Pogonia divaricata*

123 Marsh Wren
*(Telmatodytes palustris)*
ABOVE: male; BELOW, LEFT: male; BELOW, RIGHT: female

124 Short-billed Marsh Wren
*(Cistothorus platensis)*
"Nuttall's Short-billed Marsh Wren"
ABOVE: male; BELOW: female
Nest

125 Crested Titmouse
*(Parus bicolor)*
ABOVE: male; BELOW: female
PLANT: White Pine. *Pinus strobus*

126 Black Cap Titmouse
*(Parus atricapillus)*
ABOVE: male; BELOW: female
PLANT: Sweet Briar

127 Carolina Titmouse
*(Parus carolinensis)*
ABOVE: male; BELOW: female
PLANT: Supple Jack

128 Hudson's Bay Titmouse
*(Parus hudsonicus)*
ABOVE: male; BELOW, LEFT: female; BELOW, RIGHT: young

129 Chestnut-backed Titmouse
*(Parus rufescens)*
ABOVE: female; BELOW: male

130 Chestnut-crowned Titmouse
*(Psaltriparus minimus)*
ABOVE: male; BELOW: female
Nest

131 Cuvier's Kinglet
*(Regulus cuvieri)*
"Cuvier's Regulus"
Male
PLANT: Broad-leaved Laurel. *Kalmia latifolia*

132                                            133

137

142

132  American Golden-crested Kinglet
     *(Regulus satrapa)*
     "American Golden-crested Wren"
     ABOVE: female; BELOW: male
     PLANT: *Thalia dealbata*

133  Ruby-crowned Kinglet
     *(Regulus calendula)*
     "Ruby-crowned Regulus"
     ABOVE: male; BELOW: female
     PLANT: *Kalmia angustifolia*

134  Common Bluebird
     *(Sialia sialis)*
     "Blue Bird"
     ABOVE: male; BELOW, LEFT: female; BELOW, RIGHT: young
     PLANT: Great Mullein. *Verbascum thapsus*

135  Western Bluebird
     *(Sialia mexicana)*
     ABOVE: male; BELOW: female

136  Arctic Bluebird
     *(Sialia currucoides)*
     ABOVE: male; BELOW: female

137  American Dipper
     *(Cinclus mexicanus)*
     LEFT: male; RIGHT: female

138  Common Mocking Bird
     *(Mimus polyglottos)*
     "Mocking Bird"
     ABOVE AND CENTER: males; BELOW: female
     PLANT: Florida Jessamine
     Rattlesnake

139  Mountain Mocking Bird
     *(Oreoscoptes montanus)*
     Male

140  [Gray] Cat Bird
     See Havell colorplate 19

134

135

136

138

139

141

143

**141** Ferruginous Mocking Bird
*(Toxostoma rufum)*
"Ferruginous Thrush"
ABOVE: male; CENTER, LEFT AND RIGHT: males; BELOW: female

**142** American Robin, or Migratory Thrush
*(Turdus migratorius)*
ABOVE: female; CENTER, LEFT: male; CENTER, RIGHT: young;
BELOW, LEFT AND RIGHT: young
PLANT: Chestnut Oak. *Quercus primus*

**143** Varied Thrush
*(Ixoreus naevius)*
ABOVE: female; BELOW: male
PLANT: American Mistletoe. *Viscum verticillatum*

144

145

146

144 Wood Thrush
*(Hylocichla mustelina)*
ABOVE: male; BELOW: female
PLANT: Common Dogwood

145 Tawny Thrush
*(Hylocichla fuscescens)*
Male
PLANTS: *Habenaria lacera* and *Cornus canadensis*

146 Hermit Thrush
*(Hylocichla guttata)*
ABOVE: male; BELOW: female
PLANT: Robin Wood

147 Dwarf Thrush
*(Hylocichla guttata)*
Male
PLANT: *Porcelia triloba*

148 Golden-crowned Wagtail (Thrush)
*(Seiurus aurocapillus)*
"Golden-crowned Thrush"
ABOVE: female; BELOW: male
PLANT: Woody Nightshade

149 Aquatic Wood Wagtail
*(Seirus motacilla* and *Seirus noveboracensis)*
"Louisiana Waterthrush and Common Waterthrush"
PLANT: Indian Turnip

150 American Pipit or Titlark
*(Anthus spinoletta)*
"Brown Titlark"

151 Shore Lark
*(Eremophila alpestris)*

152 Lapland Lark Bunting
*(Calcarius lapponicus)*
"Lapland Longspur"
LEFT: female; CENTER: male, winter plumage; RIGHT: male, spring plumage

150

152

147

148

149

151

153 Painted Lark Bunting
 *(Calcarius pictus)*
 "Painted Bunting"
 Male

154 Chestnut-collared Lark Bunting
 *(Calcarius ornatus)*
 Male

155 Black-throated Bunting
 *(Spiza americana)*
 ABOVE: female; BELOW: male
 PLANTS: *Phalaris arundinacea* and *Autirrhinum linaria*

153

154

155

156

157

158

156 Snow Lark Bunting
*(Plectrophenax nivalis)*
"Snow Bunting"
ABOVE AND CENTER: adults; BELOW: young

157 Townsend's Bunting
*(Spiza townsendi)*
Male

158 Lark Bunting
*(Chondestes grammacus)*
"Lark Finch"
Male

159 Bay-winged Bunting
*(Pooecetes gramineus)*
"Grass Finch or Bay-winged Bunting"
Male
PLANT: Prickly Pear. *Cactus opuntia*

160 Savannah Bunting
*(Passerculus sandwichensis)*
"Savannah Finch"
ABOVE: female; BELOW: male
PLANT: Indian Pink-root. *Spigelia marilandica*

161 Clay-colored Bunting
*(Spizella pallida)*
Male
PLANT: *Asclepias tuberosa*

162 Yellow-winged Bunting
*(Ammodramus savannarum)*
"Yellow-winged Sparrow"
Male

162

163

159                       160                       161

163   Henslow's Bunting
      *(Passerherbulus henslowii)*
      Male
      PLANTS: Indian Pink-root or Worm-grass and *Phlox aristata*

164   Field Bunting
      *(Spizella pusilla)*
      "Field Sparrow"
      Male
      PLANTS: *Calopogon pulchellus* and Dwarf Huckleberry

165   Chipping Bunting
      *(Spizella passerina)*
      "Chipping Sparrow"
      Male
      PLANT: Black Locust or False Acacia. *Robinus pseudocacia*

164

165

166

167

168

173

174

175

166  Canada Bunting (Tree Sparrow)
     (*Spizella arborea*)
     ABOVE: female; BELOW: male
     PLANT: Canadian Barberry

167  Common Snow Bird
     (*Junco hyemalis*)
     "Snow Bird"
     ABOVE: female; BELOW: male

168  Oregon Snow Bird
     (*Junco oreganus*)
     "Oregon Snow-finch"
     ABOVE: female; BELOW: male
     PLANT: *Rosa laevigata*

169  Painted Bunting
     See Havell colorplate 30

170  Indigo Bunting
     (*Passerina cyanea*)
     "Indigo Bird"
     ABOVE: three males in different states of plumage;
     BELOW: female
     PLANT: Wild Sarsaparilla

171  Lazuli Finch
     (*Passerina amoena*)
     ABOVE: male; BELOW: female
     PLANT: Wild Spanish Coffee

172  Sea-side Finch
     (*Ammospiza maritima*)
     ABOVE: female; BELOW: male
     PLANT: Carolina Rose

170             171             172

176             177             178

173   Macgillivray's Shore Finch
      *(Ammospiza maritima)*
      "Macgillivray's Finch"
      ABOVE: male; BELOW: female

174   Sharp-tailed Finch
      *(Ammospiza caudacuta)*
      ABOVE AND CENTER: males; BELOW: female
      Nest

175   Swamp Sparrow
      *(Melospiza georgiana)*
      **Male**
      PLANT: May Apple

176   Bachman's Pinewood Finch
      *(Aimophila aestivalis)*
      "Bachman's Finch"
      Male
      PLANT: *Pinckneya pubescens*

177   Lincoln's Pinewood Finch
      *(Melospiza lincolnii)*
      "Lincoln's Finch"
      ABOVE: male; BELOW: female
      PLANTS: Dwarf Cornel; Cloudberry; Glaucous Kalmia

178   Mealy Redpoll Linnet
      *(Acanthis hornemanni)*
      "Mealy Redpoll"
      Male

179 Lesser Redpoll Linnet
(*Acanthis flammea*)
"Lesser Redpoll"
ABOVE: male; BELOW: female

180 Pine Linnet
(*Spinus pinus*)
"Pine Finch"
ABOVE: male; BELOW: female
PLANT: Black Larch

181 American Goldfinch
(*Spinus tristis*)
ABOVE: male; BELOW: female
PLANT: Common Thistle

182 Black-headed Goldfinch
(*Spinus notatus*)
"Black-headed Siskin"
Male

183 Arkansas Goldfinch
(*Spinus psaltria*)
"Arkansaw Siskin"
Male

184 Yarrell's Goldfinch
(*Spinus psaltria*)
"Mexican Goldfinch"
ABOVE: female; BELOW: male

185 Stanley Goldfinch
(*Carduelis stanleyi*)

186 Fox-colored Finch
(*Passerella iliaca*)
"Fox-coloured Sparrow"
LEFT: female; RIGHT: male

187 Townsend's Finch
(*Melospiza melodia*)
"Brown Song Sparrow"
Male

188 Brown Finch
(*Melospiza melodia*)
Female

189 Song Finch
(*Melospiza melodia*)
"Song Sparrow"
ABOVE: male; BELOW: female
PLANT: Huckleberry or Blue-tangled
*Vaecinium frondosum*

190 Morton's Finch
(*Brachyspiza mortoni*)
Male

191 White-throated Finch
(*Zonotrichia albicollis*)
"White-throated Sparrow"
ABOVE: female; BELOW: male
PLANT: Common Dogwood

179

180

183

184

187

188

181

182

186

185

190

191

189

192

193

196

197

198

200

201

202

194

195

199

192 White-crowned Finch
(*Zonotrichia leucophrys*)
"White-crowned Sparrow"
ABOVE: male; BELOW: female
PLANT: Wild Summer Grape

193 Black-and-yellow-crowned Finch
(*Zonotrichia atricapilla*)

194 Arctic Ground Finch
(*Pipilo erythrophthalmus*)
LEFT: female; RIGHT: male

195 Towhe Ground Finch
(*Pipilo erythrophthalmus*)
"Towhe Bunting"
ABOVE: male; BELOW: female
PLANT: Common Blackberry

196 Crested Purple Finch
(*Carpodacus purpureus*)
"Purple Finch"
ABOVE AND CENTER: males; BELOW: female
PLANT: Red Larch. *Larix americana*

197 Crimson-fronted Purple Finch
(*Carpodacus mexicanus*)
"Crimson-necked Finch"
Male

198 Gray-crowned Purple Finch
(*Leucosticte tephrocotis*)
"Grey-crowned Linnet"
Male
PLANT: *Stokesia cyanea*

199 Common Pine-finch
(*Pinicola enucleator*)
"Pine Grosbeak"
ABOVE: female; BELOW: male

200 Common Crossbill
(*Loxia curvirostra*)
ABOVE, LEFT, AND BELOW, RIGHT: females;
ABOVE, RIGHT, AND BELOW, LEFT: males

201 White-winged Crossbill
(*Loxia leucoptera*)
ABOVE, LEFT, AND BELOW, RIGHT: females;
ABOVE, RIGHT, AND BELOW, LEFT: males

202 Prairie Lark-Finch
(*Calamospiza melanocorys*)
"Prairie Finch"
ABOVE: male; BELOW: female

203 Common Cardinal Grosbeak [Cardinal]
See Havell colorplate 27

204

205

209

210

211

213

206

207

208


212

209  Scarlet Tanager
*(Piranga olivacea)*
ABOVE: male; BELOW: female

210  Louisiana Tanager
*(Piranga ludoviciana)*
ABOVE, LEFT AND RIGHT: males; BELOW: female

211  Wandering Rice-bird
*(Dolichonyx oryzivorus)*
"Rice Bird"
ABOVE: male; BELOW: female
PLANT: Red Maple. *Acer rubrum*

212  Common Cow-bird
*(Molothrus ater)*
"Cow-pen Bird"
LEFT: female; CENTER: male; RIGHT: young

213  Saffron-headed Marsh Blackbird
*(Xanthocephalus xanthocephalus)*
"Yellow-headed Troopial"
ABOVE: female; BELOW, LEFT: male; BELOW, RIGHT: young male

214  Red-and-white-shouldered Marsh Blackbird
*(Agelaius tricolor)*
"Red-and-white-winged Troopial"
Male

215  Red-and-black-shouldered Marsh Blackbird
*(Agelaius phoeniceus)*
"Crimson-winged Troopial"
ABOVE: female; BELOW: male

204  Blue Song Grosbeak
*(Guiraca caerulea)*
"Blue Grosbeak"
ABOVE: male; CENTER: young; BELOW: female

205  Rose-breasted Song Grosbeak
*(Pheucticus ludovicianus)*
"Rose-breasted Grosbeak"
ABOVE: young male; CENTER: female;
BELOW, LEFT AND RIGHT: males
PLANT: Ground Hemlock. *Taxus canadensis*

206  Black-headed Song Grosbeak
*(Pheucticus melanocephalus)*
"Black-headed Grosbeak"
ABOVE, AND BELOW, RIGHT: males; BELOW, LEFT: female

207  Evening Grosbeak
*(Hesperiphona vespertina)*
ABOVE: male; CENTER: young male; BELOW: female

208  Summer Red-bird
*(Piranga rubra)*
ABOVE: male; CENTER: female; BELOW: young male
PLANT: Wild Muscadine. *Vitis rotundifolia*

216

218

219

224

225

226

216  Red-winged Starling
 *(Agelaius phoeniceus)*
 ABOVE: adult male; BELOW, LEFT: young male; BELOW, RIGHT: female
 PLANT: Red Maple

217  [Northern] Baltimore Oriole
 See Havell colorplate 28

218  Bullock's Troopial
 *(Icterus bullockii)*
 ABOVE: young male; CENTER: female; BELOW: adult male
 PLANT: *Caprifolium flavum*

219  Orchard Oriole or Hang-nest
 *(Icterus spurius)*
 ABOVE: adult male; CENTER: young male; BELOW: female
 PLANT: Honey Locust
 Nest

220  Boat-tailed Grackle
 *(Cassidix mexicanus)*
 ABOVE: female; BELOW: male
 PLANT: Live Oak

221  Common or Purple Crow Blackbird
 *(Quiscalus quiscula)*
 "Purple Grackle"
 ABOVE: female; BELOW: male
 PLANT: Maize or Indian Corn

222  Rusty Crow Blackbird
 *(Euphagus carolinus)*
 "Rusty Grackle"
 ABOVE: young; CENTER: female; BELOW: male
 PLANT: Black Haw

220

221

222

228

229

230

223 Meadow Starling or Meadow Lark
See Havell colorplate 14

224 Raven
(Corvus corax)
Old male
PLANT: Thickshell Bark Hickory

225 Common American Crow
(Corvus brachyrhynchos)
"American Crow"
Male
PLANT: Black Walnut

226 Fish Crow
(Corvus ossifragus)
ABOVE: female; BELOW: male
PLANT: Honey Locust

227 Common [Black-billed] Magpie
See Havell colorplate 10

228 Yellow-billed Magpie
(Pica nuttalli)
Male
PLANT: Plantanus

229 Columbia Magpie or Jay
(Calocitta formosa)
Males

230 Steller's Jay
(Cyanocitta stelleri)
Male

231 Blue Jay
See Havell colorplate 8

232

235

236

240

241

242

232 Ultramarine Jay
(*Aphelocoma coerulescens*)
Adult Male

233 Florida [Scrub] Jay
See Havell colorplate 12

234 Canada [Gray] Jay
See Havell colorplate 20

235 Clarke's Nutcracker
(*Nucifraga columbiana*)
ABOVE: female; BELOW: male

236 Great American Shrike
(*Lanius excubitor*)
"Great Cinereous Shrike"
ABOVE: male; CENTER: young; BELOW: female
PLANT: *Crataegus apiifolia*

237 Loggerhead Shrike
(*Lanius ludovicianus*)
LEFT: female; RIGHT: male
PLANT: Greenbriar or Round-leaved
Smilax. *Smilax rotundifolia*

238 Yellow-throated Vireo or Greenlet
(*Vireo flavifrons*)
Male
PLANT: Swamp Snowball. *Hydrangea quercifolia*

239 Solitary Vireo or Greenlet
(*Vireo solitarius*)
"Solitary Fly-catcher"
ABOVE: male; BELOW: female
PLANT: American Cane

237

238

239

243

245

246

240 White-eyed Vireo or Greenlet
(*Vireo griseus*)
"White-eyed Fly-catcher or Vireo"
Male
PLANT: Pride of China or Bead Tree. *Melia azedarach*

241 Warbling Vireo or Greenlet
(*Vireo gilvus*)
"Warbling Flycatcher"
ABOVE: male; BELOW: female
PLANT: Swamp Magnolia

242 Bartram's Vireo or Greenlet
(*Vireo olivaceus*)
Male
PLANT: Ipomea

243 Red-eyed Vireo or Greenlet
(*Vireo olivaceus*)
Male
PLANT: Honey Locust

244 Yellow-breasted Chat
See Havell colorplate 25

245 Black-throated Wax-wing
or Bohemian Chatterer
(*Bombycilla garrulus*)
ABOVE: female; BELOW: male
PLANT: Canadian Service Tree

246 Cedarbird, or Cedar Wax-wing
(*Bombycilla cedrorum*)
ABOVE: female; BELOW: male
PLANT: Red Cedar

247

248

249

250

251

252

253

254

256

258

259

247 White-breasted Nuthatch
(*Sitta carolinensis*)
ABOVE: female; CENTER: male; BELOW: female

248 Red-bellied Nuthatch
(*Sitta canadensis*)
ABOVE: male; BELOW: female

249 Brown-headed Nuthatch
(*Sitta pusilla*)
ABOVE: female; BELOW: male

250 Californian Nuthatch
(*Sitta pygmaea*)
Adults

251 Mango Hummingbird
(*Antracothorax nigricollis*)
ABOVE: male; BELOW, LEFT: male; BELOW, RIGHT: female
PLANT: *Bignonia grandiflora*

252 Anna Hummingbird
(*Calypte anna*)
ABOVE, LEFT AND RIGHT: males; BELOW: female
PLANT: *Hibiscus virginicus*

253 Ruby-throated Hummingbird
(*Archilochus colubris*)
ABOVE, LEFT: two males; ABOVE, RIGHT: female; BELOW: young
PLANT: *Bignonia radicans*

254 Ruff-necked Hummingbird
(*Selasphorus rufus*)
ABOVE: two males; BELOW: female
PLANT: *Cleome heptaphylla*

255 Belted Kingfisher
See Havell colorplate 24

256 Ivory-billed Woodpecker
(*Campephilus principalis*)
LEFT: male; RIGHT, ABOVE AND BELOW: females

257 Pileated Woodpecker
See Havell colorplate 21

258 Canadian Woodpecker
(*Dendrocopos villosus*)
Male

259 Phillips' Woodpecker
(*Dendrocopos villosus*)
Males

260 Maria's Woodpecker
(*Dendrocopos villosus*)
ABOVE: female; BELOW: male

261

262

263

266

267

268

261 Harris' Woodpecker
*(Dendrocopos villosus)*
ABOVE: male; BELOW: female

262 Hairy Woodpecker
*(Dendrocopos villosus)*
ABOVE: male; BELOW: female

263 Downy Woodpecker
*(Dendrocopos pubescens)*
ABOVE: male; BELOW: female

264 Red-cockaded Woodpecker
*(Dendrocopos borealis)*
ABOVE: female; CENTER AND BELOW: males

265 Audubon's Woodpecker
*(Dendrocopos villosus)*
Male

266 Red-breasted Woodpecker
*(Dendrocopos villosus)*
ABOVE: female; BELOW: male

267 Yellow-bellied Woodpecker
*(Sphyrapicus varius)*
ABOVE: male; BELOW: female
PLANT: *Prunus caroliniana*

268 Arctic Three-toed Woodpecker
*(Picoïdes arcticus)*
"Three-toed Woodpecker"
ABOVE: male; CENTER: female; BELOW: male

264

265

269

270

271

269   Banded Three-toed Woodpecker
      (*Picoïdes tridactylus*)
      "Common Three-toed Woodpecker"
      ABOVE: male; BELOW: female

270   Red-bellied Woodpecker
      (*Centurus carolinus*)
      ABOVE: male; BELOW: female

271   Red-headed Woodpecker
      (*Melanerpes erythrocephalus*)
      ABOVE, LEFT: female; ABOVE, RIGHT: young; CENTER: young;
      BELOW, LEFT: male; BELOW, RIGHT: young

272   Lewis' Woodpecker
      (*Asyndesmus lewis*)
      LEFT: male; RIGHT: female

272

273  Golden-winged Woodpecker
(*Colaptes auratus*)
ABOVE AND CENTER: females;
BELOW: male

274  Red-shafted Woodpecker
(*Colaptes cafer*)
"Red-shafted Flicker"
ABOVE: female; BELOW: male

275  Yellow-billed Cuckoo
(*Coccyzus americanus*)
LEFT: female; RIGHT: male
PLANT: Pawpaw Tree

276  Black-billed Cuckoo
(*Coccyzus erythropthalmus*)
LEFT: female; RIGHT: male
PLANT: *Magnolia grandiflora*

277  Mangrove Cuckoo
(*Coccyzus minor*)
Male
PLANT: Seven-years Apple

278  Carolina Parrot or Parakeet
See Havell colorplate 15

273

274

277

280

283

275                                                                          276

282

281

279  Band-tailed Dove or Pigeon
     See Havell colorplate 2

280  White-headed Dove or Pigeon
     *(Columba leucocephala)*
     LEFT: female; RIGHT: male
     PLANT: *Cordia sebestina*

281  Zenaida Dove
     *(Zenaida aurita)*
     ABOVE: female; BELOW: male
     PLANT: Anona

282  Key West Dove
     *(Geotrygon chrysia)*
     "Key West Pigeon"
     LEFT: male; RIGHT: female

283  Ground Dove
     *(Columbigallina passerina)*
     ABOVE, LEFT AND RIGHT: males; BELOW, LEFT: female;
     BELOW, RIGHT: young
     PLANT: Wild Orange

284

288

291

292

295

296

284  Blue-headed Ground Dove or Pigeon
(*Starnoenas cyanocephala*)
"Blue-headed Pigeon"
LEFT AND CENTER: females; RIGHT: male

285  Passenger Pigeon
See Havell colorplate 7

286  Carolina Turtle Dove [Mourning Dove]
See Havell colorplate 13

287  Wild Turkey [Gobbler]
See Havell colorplate 4

288  Wild Turkey
(*Meleagris gallopavo*)
Female and young

289  Common American Partridge
(*Ortix virginiana*)
LEFT: male; CENTER: young; RIGHT: female

290  Californian Partridge
(*Lophortyx californicus*)
LEFT: female; RIGHT: male

291  Plumed Partridge
(*Oreortyx pictus*)
LEFT: male; RIGHT: female

289

290

293

294

297

298

292 Welcome Partridge
*(Colinus cristatus)*
Young

293 Ruffed Grouse
*(Bonasa umbellus)*
ABOVE, LEFT AND RIGHT: males; BELOW: female

294 Canada Grouse
*(Canachites canadensis)*
FROM LEFT: first and third, females; second and
fourth, males
PLANTS: *Trillium pictum* and *Streptopus distortus*

295 Dusky Grouse
*(Dendragapus obscurus)*
LEFT: male; RIGHT: female

296 Pinnated Grouse
*(Tympanuchus cupido)*
ABOVE, AND BELOW, RIGHT: males; BELOW, LEFT: female
PLANT: *Lilium superbum*

297 Cock of the Plains
*(Centrocercus urophasianus)*
LEFT: female; RIGHT: male

298 Sharp-tailed Grouse
*(Pedioecetes phasianellus)*
LEFT: female; RIGHT: male

299

300

302

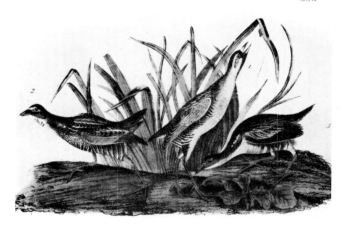

303

305

306

308

309

301

304

307

310

299 Willow Ptarmigan
*(Lagopus lagopus)*
"Willow Grous"
LEFT: male; RIGHT: female and young

300 American Ptarmigan
*(Lagopus mutus)*
"Common Ptarmigan"
Male

301 Rock Ptarmigan
*(Lagopus mutus)*
"Rock Grous"
LEFT: young in August; CENTER: female,
summer plumage; RIGHT: male in winter

302 White-tailed Ptarmigan
*(Lagopus leucurus)*
"White-tailed Grous"
Adult, in winter plumage

303 Purple Gallinule
*(Porphyrula martinica)*
Adult male, spring plumage

304 Common Gallinule
*(Gallinula chloropus)*
Adult male

305 American Coot
*(Fulica americana)*

306 Sora Rail
*(Porzana carolina)*
LEFT: female; CENTER: male; RIGHT: young

307 Yellow-breasted Rail
*(Coturnicops noveboracensis)*
Adult male in spring

308 Least Water Rail
*(Laterallus jamaicensis)*
LEFT: Adult male; RIGHT: young

309 Great Red-breasted Rail, or
Fresh-water Marsh Hen
*(Rallus elegans)*
LEFT: young; RIGHT: male adult

310 Clapper Rail or Salt-water Marsh Hen
*(Rallus longirostris)*
LEFT: female; RIGHT: male

311

312

315

316

319

320

311  Virginian Rail
    *(Rallus limicola)*
    LEFT: female; CENTER: male; RIGHT: young

312  Scolopaceous Courlan
    *(Aramus guarauna)*

313  Whooping Crane
    *(Grus americana)*
    Adult male

314  Whooping Crane
    *(Grus canadensis)*
    Young

315  Black-bellied Plover
    *(Squatarola squatarola)*
    LEFT, FOREGROUND: male; LEFT, BACKGROUND:
    young in autumn; RIGHT: nestling

316  American Golden Plover
    *(Pluvialis dominica)*
    "Golden Plover"
    ABOVE: winter plumage; BELOW, LEFT: variety
    in March; BELOW, RIGHT: summer plumage

313

314

317

318

321

322

317 Killdeer Plover
   *(Charadrius vociferus)*
   LEFT: male; RIGHT: female

318 Rocky Mountain Plover
   *(Eupoda montana)*
   Female

319 Wilson's Plover
   *(Charadrius wilsonia)*
   LEFT: female; RIGHT: male

320 American Ring Plover
   *(Charadrius hiaticula)*
   LEFT: adult male; RIGHT: young in August

321 Piping Plover
   *(Charadrius melodus)*
   LEFT: female; RIGHT: male

322 Townsend's Surf Bird
   *(Aphriza virgata)*
   Females

324

323

328

327

331

330

333

325

326

329

332

323 Turnstone
*(Arenaria interpres)*
LEFT: summer plumage; RIGHT: winter plumage

324 American Oyster-catcher
*(Haematopus palliatus)*
Male

325 Bachman's Oyster-catcher
*(Haematopus bachmani)*
Male

326 Townsend's Oyster-catcher
*(Haematopus bachmani)*
Female

327 Bartramian Sandpiper
*(Bartramia longicauda)*
FOREGROUND: male; BACKGROUND: female

328 Red-breasted Sandpiper
*(Calidris canutus)*
"Knot or Ash-coloured Sandpiper"
LEFT: summer plumage; RIGHT: winter plumage

329 Pectoral Sandpiper
*(Erolia melanotos)*
LEFT: female; RIGHT: male

330 Purple Sandpiper
*(Erolia maritima)*
LEFT: summer plumage; RIGHT: winter plumage

331 Buff-breasted Sandpiper
*(Tryngites subruficollis)*
LEFT: female; RIGHT: male

332 Red-backed Sandpiper
*(Erolia alpina)*
LEFT: winter plumage; RIGHT: summer plumage

333 Curlew Sandpiper
*(Erolia ferruginea)*
LEFT: young; RIGHT: adult male

334 Long-legged Sandpiper
*(Micropalama himantopus)*

334

335

338

341

344

336

337

339

340

342

343

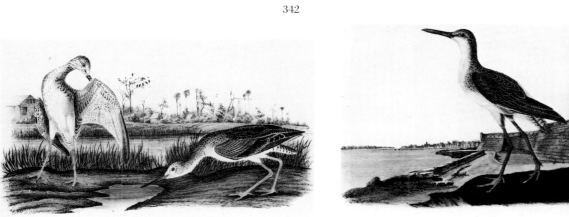

345

346

347

348

351

352

355

356

347  Semipalmated Snipe, Willet
or Stone Curlew
*(Catoptrophorus semipalmatus)*
LEFT AND CENTER: females, winter plumage;
RIGHT: male, spring plumage

348  Great Marbled Godwit
*(Limosa fedoa)*
LEFT: male, RIGHT: female

349  Hudsonian Godwit
*(Limosa haemastica)*
LEFT: female, summer plumage; RIGHT: male

350  Wilson's Snipe–Common Snipe
*(Capella gallinago)*
"American Snipe"
Plantation near Charleston, South Carolina

351  Red-breasted Snipe
*(Limnodromus griseus)*
LEFT: winter plumage; RIGHT: spring plumage

349

350

353

354

357

358

352  American Woodcock
*(Philohela minor)*
LEFT: young in autumn; ABOVE, RIGHT: female;
BELOW, RIGHT: male

353  American Avocet
*(Recurvirostra americana)*
Young in first winter plumage. Adult
in the distance

354  Black-necked Stilt
*(Himantopus mexicanus)*
Male

355  Long-billed Curlew
*(Numenius americanus)*
FOREGROUND: male; BACKGROUND: female
City of Charleston, South Carolina

356  Hudsonian Curlew
*(Numenius phaeopus)*
Male

357  Esquimaux Curlew
*(Numenius borealis)*
FOREGROUND: female; BACKGROUND: male

358  Glossy Ibis
*(Plegadis falcinellus)*
Adult male

359

360

363

364

359 Scarlet Ibis
*(Eudocimus ruber)*
LEFT: adult male; RIGHT: young, second autumn

360 White Ibis
*(Eudocimus albus)*
LEFT: adult; RIGHT: young in autumn

361 Wood Ibis
*(Mycteria americana)*
Male

362 Roseate Spoonbill
*(Ajaia ajaja)*
Male

363 Black-crowned Night Heron, or Qua-Bird
*(Nycticorax nycticorax)*
"Night Heron"
LEFT: adult; RIGHT: young

364 Yellow-crowned Night Heron
*(Nyctanassa violacea)*
"Yellow-crowned Heron"
ABOVE: young in October; BELOW: adult,
spring plumage

365 American Bittern
*(Botaurus lentiginosus)*
LEFT: male; RIGHT: female

366 Least Bittern
*(Ixobrychus exilis)*
LEFT: young; CENTER: female; RIGHT: male

367 Green Heron
*(Butorides virescens)*
LEFT: young in September; RIGHT: adult male

368 Great White Heron
*(Ardea occidentalis)*
Adult male, spring plumage

369 Great Blue Heron
See Havell colorplate 6

361

362

365

366

367

368

370

374

376

378

379

381

371

372

377

380

370 Great American White Egret
(*Casmerodius albus*)
"Great American Egret"
Male, spring plumage

371 Reddish Egret
(*Dichromanassa rufescens*)
LEFT: young in full spring plumage, two years old;
RIGHT: adult, full spring plumage

372 Blue Heron
(*Florida caerulea*)
FOREGROUND: adult male, spring plumage;
BACKGROUND: young, second year

373 Louisiana Heron
See Havell colorplate 11

374 Snowy Heron
(*Leucophoyx thula*)
Male

375 American [Greater] Flamingo
See Havell colorplate 29

376 Canada Goose
(*Branta canadensis*)
LEFT: male; RIGHT: female

377 Hutchins' Goose
(*Branta canadensis*)
Adult male

378 Barnacle Goose
(*Branta leucopsis*)
LEFT: male; RIGHT: female

379 Brant Goose
(*Branta bernicla*)
LEFT: female; RIGHT: male

380 White-fronted Goose
(*Anser albifrons*)
LEFT: male; RIGHT: female

381 Snow Goose
(*Chen hyperborea*)
LEFT: adult male; RIGHT: young female

382 Trumpeter Swan
See Havell colorplate 22

383 Trumpeter Swan
(*Olor buccinator*)
Young

384

386

389

390

395

396

384 American Swan
(Olor columbianus)
Male

385 Mallard
See Havell colorplate 26

386 Dusky Duck
(Anas rubripes)
LEFT: male; RIGHT: female

387 Brewer's Duck
(Hybrid duck)
Male

388 Gadwall Duck
(Anas strepera)
LEFT: female; RIGHT: male

389 American Widgeon
(Mareca americana)
LEFT: female; RIGHT: male

390 Pintail Duck
(Anas acuta)
LEFT: female; RIGHT: male

391 Wood Duck–Summer Duck
See Havell colorplate 23

387

388

392

394

397

396  Red-headed Duck
      (*Aythya americana*)
      LEFT: female; RIGHT: male

397  Scaup Duck
      (*Aythya affinis*)
      LEFT: male; RIGHT: female

398  Ring-necked Duck
      (*Aythya collaris*)
      LEFT: female; RIGHT: male

392  American Green-winged Teal
      (*Anas carolinensis*)
      LEFT: female; RIGHT: male

393  Blue-winged Teal
      See Havell colorplate 1

394  Shoveller Duck
      (*Spatula clypeata*)
      LEFT: male; RIGHT: female

395  Canvas-back Duck
      (*Aythya valisneriana*)
      LEFT: male; CENTER AND RIGHT: females
      View of Baltimore, Maryland

398

399 Ruddy Duck
*(Oxyura jamaicensis)*
FROM LEFT: first, male; second and fourth, young;
third, female

400 Pied Duck
*(Camptorhynchus labradorium)*
LEFT: female; RIGHT: male

401 Velvet Duck
*(Melanitta deglandi)*
LEFT: female; RIGHT: male

402 Black or Surf Duck
*(Melanitta perspicillata)*
LEFT: male; RIGHT: female

403 American Scoter Duck
*(Oidemia nigra)*
FOREGROUND: male; BACKGROUND: female

404 King Duck
*(Somateria spectabilis)*
LEFT: male; RIGHT: female

405 Eider Duck
*(Somateria mollissima)*
FOREGROUND: males; BACKGROUND: female

406 Golden-eye Duck
*(Bucephala clangula)*
LEFT: male; RIGHT: female

407 Western Duck
*(Polysticta stelleri)*
Males

408 Buffel-headed Duck
*(Bucephala albeola)*
LEFT: female; RIGHT: male

409 Harlequin Duck
*(Histrionicus histrionicus)*
ABOVE: female; BELOW, LEFT: old male;
BELOW, RIGHT: young male

410 Long-tailed Duck
*(Clangula hyemalis)*
FOREGROUND: female and young;
BACKGROUND, LEFT: male, summer plumage;
BACKGROUND, RIGHT: male, winter plumage

399

402

405

408

400

401

403

404

406

407

409

410

411

412

415

418

419

**411** Buff-breasted Merganser—Goosander
*(Mergus merganser)*
"Goosander"
LEFT: female; RIGHT: male

**412** Red-breasted Merganser
*(Mergus serrator)*
ABOVE: female; BELOW: male

**413** Hooded Merganser
*(Lophodytes cucullatus)*
LEFT: male; RIGHT: female

**414** White Merganser, Smew, White Nun
*(Mergellus albellus)*
"Smew or White Nun"
ABOVE: male; BELOW: female

**415** Common Cormorant
*(Phalacrocorax carbo)*
LEFT: female and young; RIGHT: male

**416** Double-crested Cormorant
*(Phalacrocorax auritus)*
Male

**417** Florida Cormorant
*(Phalacrocorax auritus)*
Male

**418** Townsend's Cormorant
*(Phalacrocorax penicillatus)*
Male

**419** Violet-green Cormorant
*(Phalacrocorax pelagicus)*
Female in winter

**420** American Anhinga—Snake Bird
*(Anhinga anhinga)*
LEFT: male; RIGHT: female

**421** Frigate Pelican—Man-of-War Bird
*(Fregata magnificens)*
Male

413

414

416

417

420

421

422

426

427

422 American White Pelican
*(Pelecanus erythrorhynchos)*
Male

423 Brown Pelican
See Havell colorplate 17

424 Brown Pelican
*(Pelecanus occidentalis)*
Young, first winter

425 Common Gannet
*(Morus bassanus)*
FOREGROUND: young;
BACKGROUND: adult male

426 Booby Gannet
*(Sula leucogaster)*
Male

427 Tropic Bird
*(Phaethon lepturus)*
LEFT: male; RIGHT: female

428 Black Skimmer or Shearwater
*(Rynchops nigra)*
Male

429 Cayenne Tern
*(Thalasseus maximus)*

430

424

425

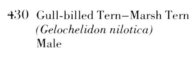

428

429

431

430 Gull-billed Tern—Marsh Tern
   (*Gelochelidon nilotica*)
   Male

431 Sandwich Tern
   (*Thalasseus sandvicensis*)
   Adult

432 Sooty Tern
   (*Sterna fuscata*)

433 Common Tern
   (*Sterna hirundo*)
   Male, spring plumage

432

434

435

440

443

434 Havell's Tern
*(Sterna forsteri)*
Adult

435 Trudeau's Tern
*(Sterna trudeaui)*
Adult

436 Arctic Tern
See Havell colorplate 3

437 Roseate Tern
*(Sterna dougallii)*
Male

438 Black Tern
*(Chlidonias niger)*
ABOVE: young; BELOW: adult

439 Least Tern
*(Sterna albifrons)*
ABOVE: young; BELOW: adult in spring

440 Noddy Tern
*(Anoüs stolidus)*
Male

441 Fork-tailed Gull
*(Xema sabini)*
Male

442 Bonaparte's Gull
*(Larus philadelphia)*
"Bonapartian Gull"
LEFT: female; RIGHT, FOREGROUND: young, first autumn;
RIGHT, BACKGROUND: male in spring

443 Black-headed Gull
*(Larus atricilla)*
"Black-headed, or Laughing Gull"
FOREGROUND: adult male, spring plumage;
BACKGROUND: young, first autumn

444 Kittiwake Gull
*(Rissa tridactyla)*
FOREGROUND: adult; BACKGROUND: young

445 Ivory Gull
*(Pagophila eburnea)*
LEFT: adult male; RIGHT: young, second autumn

437

438

439

441

442

444

445

446

447

451

452

446 Common American Gull–Ring-billed Gull
(*Larus delawarensis*)
LEFT: adult; RIGHT: young

447 White-winged Silvery Gull
(*Larus glaucoides*)
ABOVE: young in winter; BELOW: male in summer

448 Herring or Silvery Gull
(*Larus argentatus*)
ABOVE: adult in spring; BELOW: young in autumn

449 Glaucous Gull or Burgomaster
(*Larus hyperboreus*)
LEFT: adult male; RIGHT: young, first autumn

450 Great Black-backed Gull
(*Larus marinus*)
Male

451 Pomerine Jager
(*Stercorarius pomarinus*)
Adult female

452 Richardson's Jager
(*Stercorarius parasiticus*)
LEFT: adult male; RIGHT: young in September

453 Arctic Jager
(*Stercorarius longicaudus*)

455

456

449

448

454 Dusky Albatross
   (*Phoebetria palpebrata*)

455 Fulmar Petrel
   (*Fulmarus glacialis*)
   Adult male, summer plumage

456 Wandering Shearwater
   (*Puffinus gravis*)
   Male

457 Manks Shearwater
   (*Puffinus puffinus*)
   Male

458 Dusky Shearwater
   (*Puffinus lherminieri*)
   "Dusky Petrel"
   Male in spring

450

453

454

457

458

459

460

463

464

467

468

459 Leach's Petrel—Forked-tailed Petrel
(*Oceanodroma leucorhoa*)
LEFT: female; RIGHT: male

460 Wilson's Petrel—Mother Carey's Chicken
(*Oceanites oceanicus*)
LEFT: male; RIGHT: female

461 Least Petrel—Mother Carey's Chicken
(*Hydrobates pelagicus*)
LEFT: female; RIGHT: male

462 Tufted Puffin
(*Lunda cirrhata*)
LEFT: female; RIGHT: male

463 Large-billed Puffin
(*Fratercula corniculata*)
LEFT: male; RIGHT: female

464 Common or Arctic Puffin
(*Fratercula arctica*)
"Puffin"
LEFT: female; RIGHT: male

465 Great Auk
(*Pinguinus impennis*)
Adult

466 Razor-billed Auk
(*Alca torda*)
LEFT: female; RIGHT: male

467 Curled-crested Phaleris
(*Aethia cristatella*)
Adult

461

462

465

466

469

470

471

**468** Knobbed-billed Phaleris
*(Aethia pusilla)*
Adult

**469** Little Auk—Sea Dove
*(Plautus alle)*
"Little Guillemot"
LEFT: female; RIGHT: male

**470** Black-throated Guillemot
*(Synthliboramphus antiquum)*
LEFT: adult; RIGHT: young

**471** Horned-billed Guillemot
*(Cerorhinca monocerata)*
Adult

472

473

475

476

478

479

481

482

474

472 Large-billed Guillemot
(*Uria lomvia*)
Male

473 Foolish Guillemot—Murre
(*Uria aalge*)
LEFT: female; RIGHT: male

474 Black Guillemot
(*Cepphus grylle*)
ABOVE: adult in winter; BELOW, LEFT: young;
BELOW, RIGHT: adult in summer

475 Slender-billed Guillemot
(*Brachyramphus marmoratum*)
LEFT: female; RIGHT: male

476 Great North Diver or Loon
(*Gavia immer*)
LEFT: young in winter; RIGHT: adult

477 Black-throated Diver
(*Gavia arctica*)
LEFT: male; CENTER: young in October; RIGHT: female

478 Red-throated Diver
(*Gavia stellata*)
FROM LEFT: male, winter plumage; young; female;
male, summer plumage

479 Crested Grebe
(*Podiceps cristatus*)
LEFT: young, first winter; RIGHT: adult male, spring

480 Red-necked Grebe
(*Podiceps grisegena*)
LEFT: adult male, spring plumage;
RIGHT: young, winter plumage

481 Horned Grebe
(*Podiceps auritus*)
LEFT: adult male; RIGHT: female in winter

482 Eared Grebe
(*Podiceps caspicus*)
LEFT: male; RIGHT: young, first year

483 Pied-billed Dobchick
(*Podilymbus podiceps*)
LEFT: female; RIGHT: male

477

480

483

484 Harris' Finch
*(Zonotrichia querula)*
ABOVE: adult male; BELOW: young female

485 Bell's Vireo
*(Vireo belli)*
Male
PLANT: Rattlesnake Root

486 Sprague's Missouri Lark
*(Anthus spraguei)*
Male

487 Smith's Lark Bunting
*(Calcarius pictus)*
Adult male

488 Le Conti's Sharp-tailed Bunting
*(Passerherbulus caudacutus)*
Male

489 Missouri Meadow Lark
*(Sturnella neglecta)*
Male

490 Yellow-bellied Flycatcher
*(Empidonax flaviventris)*
Male

491 Least Flycatcher
*(Empidonax minimus)*
Male

492 Brewer's Blackbird
*(Euphagus cyanocephalus)*
Male

493 Shattuck's Bunting
*(Spizella pallida)*
Male

494 Missouri Red-moustached Woodpecker
(Hybrid flicker)
Male

495 Nuttall's Whip-poor-will
*(Phalaenoptilus nuttalli)*
Male

484

485

488

489

493

494

486

487

490

491

492

495

496

497

498

499

500

496  The Texan Turtle Dove
    *(Melopelia asiatica)*
    Male

497  Western Shore Lark
    *(Otocoris alpestris)*
    Male

498  Common Scaup Duck
    *(Nyroca marila)*
    LEFT: male; RIGHT: female

499  Common Troopial
    *(Icterus icterus)*
    Male

500  Baird's Bunting
    *(Ammodramus bairdi)*
    Male

# INDEX
# OF
# ILLUSTRATIONS

All numbers in this index
refer to plate numbers in
the illustrated catalogue
except for those preceded
by the word "Havell," which
designate plates in the section
"Thirty Great Audubon Birds."
Asterisks denote colorplates.

## A

Albatross, dusky, 454
Anhinga, American, 420
Auk, great, 465
    little, 469
    razor-billed, 466
Avocet, American, 353

## B

Bittern, American, 365
    least, 366
Blackbird, Brewer's, 492
    common or purple crow, 221
    red-and-black-shouldered marsh, 215
    red-and-white-shouldered marsh, 214
    rusty crow, 222
    saffron-headed marsh, 213
Bluebird, Arctic, 136
    common, 134
    western, 135
Bunting, Baird's, 500
    bay-winged, 159
    black-throated, 155
    Canada, 166
    chestnut-collared lark, 154
    chipping, 165
    clay-colored, 161
    field, 164
    Henslow's 163
    indigo, 170
    Lapland lark, 152
    lark, 158
    Le Conti's sharp-tailed, 488

painted, 169; Havell *30
painted lark, 153
Savannah, 160
Shattuck's, 493
Smith's lark, 487
snow lark, 156
Townsend's, 157
yellow-winged, 162
Burgomaster, 449
Buzzard, broad-winged, 10; Havell *18
    common, 6
    Harlan's, 8
    Harris', 5
    red-shouldered, 9
    red-tailed, 7
    rough-legged, 11

## C

Cardinal, 203; Havell *27
Cat bird, 140; Havell *19
Cedarbird, 246
Chat, yellow-breasted, 244; Havell *25
Chatterer, Bohemian, 245
Chicken, Mother Carey's, 460, 461
Chuck-will's widow, 41
Cock of the Plains, 297
Coot, American, 305
Cormorant, common, 415
    double-crested, 416
    Florida, 417
    Townsend's, 418
    violet-green, 419
Courlan, scolopaceous, 312
Cow-bird, common, 212
Crane, whooping, 313, 314
Crossbill, common, 200
    white-winged, 201
Crow, carrion, 3
    common American, 225
    fish, 226
Cuckoo, black-billed, 276
    mangrove, 277

yellow-billed, 275
Curlew, esquimaux, 357
    Hudsonian, 356
    long-billed, 355
    stone, 347

## D

Dipper, American, 137
Diver, black-throated, 477
    great north, 476
    red-throated, 478
Dobchick, pied-billed, 483
Dove, band-tailed, 279; Havell *2
    blue-headed ground, 284
    Carolina turtle, 286; Havell *13
    ground, 283
    Key West, 282
    mourning, 286; Havell *13
    sea, 469
    Texan turtle, 496
    white-headed, 280
    Zenaida, 281
Duck, American scoter, 403
    black, 402
    Brewer's, 387
    buffel-headed, 408
    canvas-back, 395
    common scaup, 498
    dusky, 386
    eider, 405
    gadwall, 388
    golden-eye, 406
    harlequin, 409
    king, 404
    long-tailed, 410
    pied, 400
    pintail, 390
    red-headed, 396
    ring-necked, 398
    ruddy, 399
    scaup, 397
    shoveller, 394